A History of Education in East Africa

J. C. Ssekamwa
S. M. E. Lugumba

Fountain Publishers

Fountain Publishers
P.O. Box 488
Kampala

ISBN 9970 02 241 5

Contents

Contents   iii

Preface   v

Introduction   vi

Part One: Development of Education in Kenya 1900-1963
1. From Pioneer Missions to Kikuyu Independent Schools 1900-1929   2
2. Administration, Control and Supervision of Education 1924-1939   11
3. Education in the War Period 1939-1945   16
4. The Era of the Beecher Ten-Year Development Plan 1949-1963   21
5. Agriculture and Technical Education   26
6. Racialism in Education and Inequality in Facilities for Education 31
7. Teacher Education and Types of Teachers   36

Part Two: Development of Education in Uganda 1900-1962
8. Pioneer Work of the Missionaries 1900-1925   40
9. Government Begins to Participate Directly in Uganda's Education   47
10. Education in the Period 1939-1945   54
11. Policy, Administration, Control and Development 1945-1962   58
12. The Development of Agricultural and Technical Education   65
13. Segregation in Education and the Rise of Private Schools   72
14. Disparities in the Education System   75
15. Teachers Struggle to Better their Position   79

Part Three: Development of Education in Tanganyika 1900 – 1961
16. From German Administration Days to the Dar-es-Salaam
    Education Conference 1900 – 1925   85
17. Development in Education after the 1925 Dar-es-Salaam
    Conference up to 1939   89
18. The Isherwood Committee Probes: Two Questions raised
    in 1939 Concerning Education Developments up to 1960   99
19. Criticism of the pre-Independence Education System Under
    British Administration   107
20. How Agriculture Education failed   114

Part Four: Development of Education in Zanzibar 1900 -1920
21. Education in Zanzibar 1900-1920   118
22. Searching for an Education Policy 1920 - 1940   124
23. Zanzibar's Structure of Education and its Development Under
    the British Administration 1930 - 1963   128

Part Five: Development of Education since Independence
24. Kenya   140
25. Uganda   148
26. Tanganyika (Tanzania After 1964)   161
27. Higher Education 1922-1970   164
28. Miscellaneous and Conclusion   174

References   179
Index   181

Preface to First Edition

Even within the compass of this book we have found it absolutely imperative to quote and not to paraphrase statements on policy, purpose and status of Education by the people who were engaged in operating the education system. While we very much appreciate their dedication to the task, their sincerity and diligence, it would be incorrect on our part to shy away from commenting on the shortcomings of the system they were responsible for. There is no attempt in the book to criticize an individual as such all the comments we have made are in connection with policy task, or duty each was associated with.

It has been gratifying to us to find when studying developments since independence that contrary to what some key people in the colonial days thought, East Africans on their own, with their own policies and within limits imposed by resources, have in the short span of time achieved unbelievable peaks in educational development. In 1960 the question was how to get an adequate number of people with full secondary education to meet our requirements. Today the question is what to do with large numbers of people with secondary school education and higher qualifications. To us, the availability of such people should not be viewed as a problem but as a source of manpower to be usefully utilised in national development. We refuse to be party to the fears expressed in some quarters that large numbers having of unemployed graduates could bring about social upheaval.

We confidently think that East Africa is in good standing now and that what we have to do is, not stand by the road side or sit in conference and wail over the large numbers of educated people but look for ways of utilising this invaluable resource of manpower. To be able to do this, it is time we relied less and less on experimenters and advisors of foreign origin. Let us sit down ourselves and get to work, and think of ways to use human resources that have been made available and further decide what we want our education system to do.

We express our indebtedness to sources we have used in writing this account to the professional encouragement given to us by the Head of our Department, Professor A. Wandira.

J.C. Ssekamwa & S. M. E. Lugumba
Makerere University
1973

Preface to Second Edition

A History of Education in East Africa examines the differenct approaches that
have been used to establish western education in East Africa. This book is divided
into five sections.The first four deal with development of education in Kenya,
Uganda, Tanganyika and Zanzibar from 1900-1963. Section five gives a comparative
analysis of education in East Africa since independence.

The book looks into the pioneering work of missionaries in education and the
direct involvement of the governments. It examines policy administration, control,
supervision and development of education. This book examines education in its
wide context of teacher education, agriculture and technical education, and
higher education. This book discusses the major problems and challenges such
as racialism and inequality that faced various stakeholders in the management of
education in the region

This is an authoritative book on the development of education in East Africa
and is a sound foundation for the study of comparative education   education in
East Africa from a historical perspective.

J.C. Ssekamwa
Makerere University
2001

Introduction

It would be an unpardonable blunder and a display of shallowness of one's knowledge of the history of educational development in East Africa, to suggest that education started with the beginnings of contact with aliens, for example, Arabs, Portuguese and the British. Some foreign writers have not been able to avoid making this blunder, for instance, Keith Cole the author of "Kenya Hanging in the Middle Way" bluntly states:

> Education was first brought to the Africans by the Christian Missionary agencies, C.M.S. always being foremost in this vital work[1].

There is no need to comment at length on the statement, which has no element of truth in it. Indigenous traditional education systems existed for hundreds of years. Indeed scholarship has brought to light the seriousness and thoroughness, of these educational systems, and the *Harambee* spirit that propelled it through changing conditions.

It is, therefore, important to point out that the account of educational developments that follows here and all accounts elsewhere in this book are in the name of selectivity (one of the pillars of historical writing), related to the new foreign school system. This was the system that was and is still regulated by ordinances, and characterised by organised classes with limited number of children, in attendance at school for specific hours during the day, and learning a specified number of subjects taught by certain qualified teachers. It is an indisputable fact that we East Africans have accepted it although we can now proudly say that the power to modify it to suit our needs, other things being equal, lies entirely in our hands.

J.C. Ssekamwa & S.M.E. Lugumba

PART ONE

DEVELOPMENT OF EDUCATION IN KENYA 1900-1963

1

From Pioneer Missions to Kikuyu Independent Schools 1900-1929

Education for African Kenyans, particularly in the early part of this period, is indissolubly bound up with missionary work. At the beginning of 1900, the missionaries (Christians particularly) had been in the field for half a century promoting the new system of education by establishing schools in many places of Kenya. The story Dr. Ludwig Krapf and J. Erhardt of the Church Missionary Society setting up the first school at the coast in 1884, has often been told in history books and should be familiar to the reader. To this event may be added the opening up of Church Missionary Society schools in Freetown, West Africa in 1875 for freed slaves, at Sagala (Taita) Kenya in 1882, and Taveta in 1890. At the same time, other partners in the task of establishing the schools were active. Firstly, the United Methodist Mission had schools at Ribe, Jomvu, Lamu and Golbanti. Secondly, the Church of Scotland Mission, encouraged by the director of the Imperial British East African Company, William Mackinnon, a Scotsman, worked in Kikuyu area from 1889. Thirdly, the Roman Catholic Holy Ghost Fathers in 1892 opened a station in Mombasa and also at Bura in Taita Hills. Fourthly, the African inland Mission worked in Ukambani area at Nzaui in 1895. It is noteworthy that one of the first pupils of this mission was one of the three African Kenyans sent to England in connection with the question of the federation of East Africa in 1931.

Missionaries had schools in many parts of Kenya by 1910

In 1900 the Church Missionary Society which had began its work in the Highlands in 1898 opened a school at Kabete. The Kahuhia, Weithanga, and Embu centres were later developments of this society's work.

There were also developments on an extensive scale in the west. The Nyanza Province was opened up both from the east and west. The missionaries from Uganda established Maseno, which became a very famous education centre. The Friends of Africa Mission, starting in 1902, were active in the area from Kaimosi to Mount Elgon. One of the missionaries of this subsequently started the Lumbwa Mission in Kericho in 1905. The Mill Hill Fathers began their work among the Nyanza Province people in 1904, which was to extend in later years from Mumias to Kisii.

Other missions which entered the Nyanza Province in these years were the African Institute of the Church of God at Bunyore in 1906, the Nilotic Independent Mission and the Seventh Day Adventists.

The Consolata Fathers, having started work early in the century at Nyeri and Limuru, extended their activities to Fort Hall and Kabaa on the Athi river in the Ukumba County. At the end of 1910 the missionaries of many denominations had established schools throughout Kenya. It has been said that they did so without any help from the Government. The director of education in his annual report, 1931, dismissed this as untrue when he wrote:

> Government from the start whether functioning through the Imperial British East Africa Company or through the Foreign Office, has consistently given help direct or indirect to missions engaged in African education, either by way of land grants or money grants. [2]

But surprisingly it is very rare that the help given to early missionaries by Africans in Kenya is mentioned. Africans may not have given financial help, but they provided labour, chiefs or leaders in village communities and offered land for a school to be built.

The Protestant Mission board of education

The Protestant missions co-operated among themselves and set up a board of education to direct their educational activities and formulate a policy. In 1909 these missions called a United Missionary Conference for Protestant Missions in Kenya. At this conference the board of education presented a scheme of elementary education for Kenyan schools which the Government of Kenya adopted later. To prevent duplication of efforts the conference separated evangelisation work from school work and demarcated spheres of operation for each mission to prevent meaningless competition.

Government's direct participation in Kenya's education

The arrival of European settlers in Kenya from 1903 onwards who were anxious to see children well taught, made Kenya's colonial government to consider participating seriously in Kenya's education system. The government neither had a policy nor a development plan or an organizational plan to guide its participation in a field where missions had gained extensive and informed experience particularly the education for Kenyans. It was felt in government circles that a survey of Kenya's education should be made by an educationist who should also recommend how the system could be organised and what type of education to give to different racial groups when government participation began.

Professor J. Nelson Fraser who had gained wide educational experience in India was invited in 1908 to perform this task.

The Fraser recommendations

In his report Fraser recommended that,

1. A department of education be set up and a director of education appointed.
2. There should be three branches of education, viz., European, Asian and African.
3. Academic type of education be given to European and Asian children.
4. For African children emphasis be put on industrial and agricultural education; the government would give grants–in–aid to missionaries for their promotion.

Response and reaction to Fraser's recommendations

The government welcomed the suggestions and set up a department of education and appointed Mr. J. R. Orr the first Director of Education in March 1911. Soon thereafter, the government opened up and operated a number of industrial and agricultural schools of which the most prominent were Machakos in 1915, Kabete and Narok in Masai land in 1919. It is noteworthy that the government when building schools, tried to do so in areas not effectively served by the missionaries.

But the missions did not entirely agree with Fraser's proposal of giving a predominantly industrial and agricultural kind of education to African children. They were thinking in terms of setting up high schools for the sons of chiefs like in Uganda to provide literate administrators and clerks. They even resisted government's insistence on running schools for Africans on Fraser's recommendations. This battle was finally resolved in 1918 at an educational conference called by the government for all representatives of the different races to present their views as to what kind of education should be given to their children. The government was persuaded to accept the idea that any efficiently run school should be eligible for grants-in-aid even if it was not an industrial school.

Types of Schools Before 1924

1. Village Schools

By 1920 at the base, the school system consisted of a very large number of schools grouped together under the general name of village schools. Many of these were mainly catechumane, where little secular instruction was given. But the general tendency was towards the introduction of more and more general instructions so that the catechumane centre became a village school eventually. All these village schools in general had four forms. Their rapid increase did not find favour with the government, for there was a tendency by the missionaries to include in the instructions as much literary education as possible while the official policy was to see to it that agriculture and technical instructions were given to the African children. Government officials did not hesitate to censure them. Thus the senior commissioner for native affairs, in his annual report for 1924, had no pleasant things to say about village schools. He wrote:

> I fear the tendency for these schools is to evolve a bad reputation of a European rather than a good specimen of a native. Mission adherents are inclined to consider themselves a class apart and to some extent outside the authority of native laws and customs. They are also apt to despise manual labour, preferring work as Clerks or Teachers to that of Agricultural Labourers! [3]

2. Central schools

Above the village schools were the central schools which aimed at the completion of the primary school course. These provided a general education leading up to a course of teacher training, a general education leading up to a secondary school, and a combined course of general and vocational instruction with an increasingly definite technical bias leading up to the two years' course at the industrial training depot of Kabete. At each stage there were always fewer girls than boys for reasons mentioned in one of the chapters of this book and which we shall not repeat here.

3. Jeanes School at Kabete

The government policy to teach Africans as future cultivators and simple tradesmen in their home areas brought about the creation of the Jeanes Teachers School at Kabete. This school would produce lowly educated teachers who would usually be married couples. After their course they were expected to live with their people in the villages and work with them. The women teachers would work with the wives of the men of the villages, teaching them child care, sanitation and other domestic skills required in rural areas.

But the general attitude of the people was against the agricultural and industrial kind of education. They looked at the policy as intended to make them peasants in a modern economy and distinct and far below the Europeans and Asians. And indeed this was the main intention of the government's policy according to which these groups had to play different roles in the Kenya society. The Africans, however, would not accept it. Their great wish for education proceeded from both an entirely great desire for general progress and enlightenment, and from a natural distaste for being under the whites and Asians.

The parents felt that changes were occurring and that they were to educate their sons soon if they were to face and survive the changing conditions of their lives. Indeed, the history of education in the whole of East Africa has shown a rejection of agricultural and industrial education by the parents and children alike, despite the fact that educationists and administrators alike have insisted that the salvation of the people was in giving the majority this type of education, since it was the main source of employment to the people. Unfortunately, especially in the case of Kenya , this kind of education tended to make the white man suspected of keeping down Africans. Official statements made at the time indicate some other grossly misleading reasons why administrators insisted on agricultural and industrial education. In his annual report for 1926, for example, the director of education stated:

> ...... A study of the examination results attached to this report show how few of the Africans have at present the power of thought which is required for a high standard of literary education. Generally speaking, the African mind in Kenya has reached the stage of sense perception. The imagination and the emotions are both highly developed but the development of the reasoning faculties must be slow. Just as handwork has been found useful in the training of mentally defective children, so the most useful training which the African can receive in his present condition is continual contact with material processes. The discipline imposed by the exactness required in joinery, carpentry, building smithing, etc., increases the power of perception and gradually develops the process of thought. Increasing emphasis is, therefore, being placed on education in Kenya in contact with material processes such as agriculture, handicrafts, sanitation, hygiene, house work, the management of money, clothing, etc. and the classroom will become more a place where the ideas and thoughts arising from practical experience can be coordinated and re-applied. By the recalling of practical work in the classroom, the laws of arithmetic, geometry, causation etc., are vividly impressed on the mind. The training of the African mind, therefore, in its present stage of development, is more dependent upon the practical than the literary arts. [4]

The white man's children were being given another kind of education and the Africans saw what it meant to get that kind of education. Though the settlers were farmers and prosperous, the Africans thought agricultural education could not easily see themselves becoming prosperous like the white settlers who were being given very large tracts of land, big loans to run their farms and many ancillary aids in their agricultural endeavours. They also employed numerous Africans on these farms at a monthly wage of 8 shillings for each labourer.

The influence of Phelps-Stokes Commission (1924) on government participation in African education

Members of the Phelps-Stokes Commission visited Kenya in 1924. The commission's terms of reference are detailed under development of education in Uganda which is described later in this book what I would like to mention here is the influence of its recommendations on government participation in African education in Kenya. The commission, having found out that colonial government's aid to missionaries who mainly shouldered the huge task of providing formal education for Africans was meagre, recommended that increased grants-in-aid be given to schools. It so happened the recommendation was made at the same time as the British Government announced its policy one Education in Tropical Africa and was therefore implemented in accordance with provisions of grants-in-aid rules 1925.

According to these rules the government accepted the principle of aiding mission schools without specifying the nature of the schools to be aided and also without specifying where aid from local native councils would be concentrated. What happened in practice was that over the years money from government tended to be a fixed sum, which had to be spent on educational institutions of various academic attainments. And local native council funds, on the other hand, tended to be spent on building schools of all nature and aiding them. By 1930, government aid had ceased to be adequate due to the many schools which had been set up since 1925. The 1934 grant-in-aid rules spelled out all nature of schools to be aided. All schools were given grants-in-aid once the director was satisfied that they had met the department of education requirements.

Local native councils, which had built junior secondary schools, lost them to the government and they were told to concentrate their aid on primary schools in the villages.

Local native councils' participation in establishing schools

Local native councils with a forward looking insight realised that the only way future adults could talk on equal terms with both the settlers and the Asians was to give a sound literary education to the young. So they went out of their way to aid the missionaries set up schools in many places of Kenya, giving them physical labour and financial support which was additional to the financial contribution given by the colonial administration to missionary schools.

In the 1920s the local native councils, inspired by African public opinion, started to feel that the mission schools were enough and needed to be increased in number by the government establishing schools. This feeling and demand was also encouraged by the dislike which Africans began to feel towards mission schools which discouraged many African cultural practices which the Africans felt were embodiment of their social strength and identity. To back up this public demand, the local native councils were all the time asking the government to come in and establish schools which were free from mission control. They even began depositing money with government on an annual basis, waiting for permission to set up their own schools. They hoped that such schools would concentrate only on giving secular education and would leave alone people's cultures to be practised in their homes as they saw fit. Moreover, it was felt that missionaries were not financially able to offer secondary education which people were beginning to demand for their sons from the mid – 1920s.

The government policy at that time was to let the missions carry on as they saw fit and for the government to build schools in only those areas where the missions had not yet begun their educational activities. This was intended to prevent duplication of services where manpower was so scarce and also fear of antagonizing the missions, which did not like to see secular control established over schools. The missions thought that it would be difficult for them to keep in touch with their pupils once schools were taken out of their own control. But the government eventually began to take notice of the demands to set up more schools in fear that the situation might get out of hand. Writing in 1929, the senior commissioner for native affairs spelt out this fear when he stated:

> The mind of the natives is swayed this way and that way; he imposes upon himself a local native rate to raise money for education purposes and perhaps offers some of this money to the missions. Some missions on their part suddenly inform him that they will have nothing to do with him unless he adopted his old time customs especially in connection with circumcision of women. The native, therefore, turns to the government for assistance and offers his money for the erection of government schools but is informed that it is not the policy of government to build government schools in areas already served by schools conducted by one of the recognized missionary bodies.

> The position so created is a difficult one and delicate one. There is a real danger that the native may in desperation resolve to build schools of his own, uncontrolled either by government or by the missions, which may easily become hotbeds of ill-informed political and anti-government propaganda.

Gradually, the government began to accept some demands from Local Native councils to set up schools themselves which would be free from mission control and by the 1940 such schools were on the increase.

The beginning of independent schools

Independent schools in Kenya developed at an early period in the development of education under the missionaries. These began in Nyanza area pioneered by John Owalo before 1910, having created his Nomiya Luo Mission, as a separatist church from the Anglican Church. The mission built churches and schools free from missionary control. John Owalo's schools came to fill in a gap that existed in this area where only a few regular missionary schools existed.

In the Gem Location, during the First World War, Odera Akongo formed his independent schools having also broken off from Anglican Church. The organisation of these schools was not too hostile to missionary education. Their leaders wanted to offer a service which could not have been otherwise offered by scarcity of mission schools and also the movement sprang from the desire of the leaders to create their own churches and teach their brothers in a manner that most appealed to their senses through Christianity.

Though the independent schools in Nyanza continued up to the 1950s, when they finally surrendered themselves to the local native administration, they did not make headlines in the history of Kenya. It was the independent schools, which began later in Kikuyu, that mostly came to the forefront. And when one mentions the subject of independent schools in Kenya, people tend to forget that there were other independent schools outside the Kikuyu area.

The Rise and Progress of the Kikuyu Independent Schools Movement

The independent schools in Kikuyu began their development in the early 1920s from two motives. The leaders in this area felt that the mission schools were not likely to give stress to the Kikuyu customs, which were the embodiment of their strength and pride. Both the African Inland Mission and the Church of Scotland Mission working in this area, were engaged in a battle to discourage many Kikuyu customs. So many Kikuyu people felt that to prevent this attack on their time-old customs, the government should have built schools and kept out the missions. The government, as we have already seen, was not prepared to do so out of fear for mission hostility.

Secondly, by the 1920s pressure groups had begun to emerge in Kenya trying to challenge the hegemony of the white man. This could not be done successively if only mission schools provided education. Some people began thinking of developing their own independent schools free from government and mission control. As a result, the Kikuyu independent schools began to develop in Kikuyu but the final recognition of the movement was in 1929 when the owners formally broke away from association with the Church of Scotland Mission.

The movement became very strong, getting many supporters from the community and many mission boys deserting mission schools to attend these schools. Of course there was plenty of objections to these schools by the missions, calling them inefficient and likely to breed undesirable characters in the community, but this condemnation did not deter the development.

As a result of disagreements among its operators, one independent school movement broke into two organisations in 1937 namely, the Kikuyu Independent Schools Association and the Kikuyu Kiringa Education Association. The latter was more opposed to any semblance of co-operation with the government, while the former did not oppose this, so long as such co-operation did not take away its independence of planning its educational activities.

The government, unlike the missions, did not condemn these schools openly. It tried to secure co-operation with their owners and eventually set apart an inspector of schools and four itinerant teachers to work with them. Speaking of these schools the director of education in 1937, said:

> Such an organisation of schools, run by the Kikuyu themselves for their own people, is potentially a most valuable educational agency. There should be in it that extra spur of keenness engendered by a spirit of what might almost be called nationalism, which must be lacking in external organisation![6]

The split in the original Kikuyu educational association did not deter the movement from setting up schools rapidly and firmly nor were the two associations exclusive of each other. In 1939 then the Kikuyu Independent Schools Association set up a teachers college at Githunguri in Kiambu District, with Peter Koinange MA as headmaster, the college supplied teachers to both groups. So in the 1940s several organisations existed to supply educational facilities to the Kenya youngsters: the missions, the local native councils, the government and the independent schools.

2

Administration, Control and Supervision of Education 1924-1939

The 1924 Educational Ordinance

The 1924 Educational Ordinance empowered the government to develop, control and supervise education in all Kenya. The ordinance further provided for the establishment of three central advisory committees to deal with European, Indian and African education. The committees, once constituted, handled business which ranged from submitting recommendations on the standardisation of African dialects to advising on the division of the colony into school areas and on reducing schoolboys' holidays. The committees had services of outstanding men from government and mission organisations whose representation on the committees was in preponderance. There was not, at least in the period 1926-1933, a black Kenyan on the Central Advisory Committee for African Education.

The Education Department Administered and Supervised Kenya's Education System

By December 31 1927, an education department manned by a director of education, a chief inspector of school, a supervisor of technical education, four inspectors of schools plus headquarters clerical staff, administered and supervised Kenya's education school system. The inspectors' detailed annual reports and their comments on problems encountered make one thing clear that they were extremely hard-working men and seriously observant. Particular mention must be made here, we feel, of Inspector G. Ernest Webb, of Nyanza Province who, in his report for 1927, hit upon the problem that sometimes made the making of a satisfactory African education policy difficult and which caused dissatisfaction with the education system among Africans. Webb observed that when native African education was discussed, the aims of the three controlling factors were not alike. The administrator's aim was peace, submissiveness, and economic development in the reserve; that of the settler, cheap labour on the farm; that of the missionaries, additional converts to his denomination. The Kenyan, on the other hand, was not after education that would serve the interests of the settler and the administrator or even those of the missionary. He was not after education that would make him remain a peasant in a modern economy and dominated by alien immigrants to Kenya.

The Kenyan, in short, wanted education that would give him power and prestige and dignity and self-sufficiency. The origin of the 'gradualist policy', it seems, could be associated with the three points of view mentioned above. The administrator, the settler and the missionaries were not keen on the rapid promotion of education for Africans lest the new knowledge leads them to seek political and economic rights or question the teaching of the missionaries. The "gradualist policy' made the African impatient.

It rightly aroused his indignant reaction when it was pursued for so many years. Looking back now, and on the basis of evidence available, it may be stated that one of the sources of the weakness of the colonial educational administrators for the most of and up to 1939, was their unwillingness to take Africans into partnership at the source when formulating and executing educational policy, plans and administration.

It was not until 1936 that two Africans were made members of the Advisory Council on African Education. Missionaries, it was believed, adequately represented the interests of the Africans. The assumption that the missionaries knew the mind and educational needs of the Africans was based on extremely sweeping grounds. Did missionaries, for example, sincerely know the aspirations of the Africans? If so, what steps did they take to cater for them in the school system, which they (the missionaries) dominated?

Also, the assumption for a long time that only Europeans were competent to run the school system both as teachers, administrators and supervisors, was also wrong. Whenever one tries to point out that educational development was slow, one is quickly told this was because of shortage of staff at Headquarters, and in the field; and of course staff means European staff. If there had been programmes to give capable Africans (and they existed) proper education training, there would not be the shortage so often quoted.

Ordinances for the Administration, Control and Supervision of Education

The first of these was the 1931 Education Ordinance important in that, under its provision rules concerning the payment of grants-in-aid of secondary schools for Kenyans were spelt out in detail. There are three things to note. First the rules cited as, "the Education (Grants-in-aid of Secondary School for Africans) rules, 1931" committed the government to grants-in-aiding secondary education for Kenyans. Second, payment of the grants-in-aid was on a scale made with reference to pupil's attendances. For example, for boarding school pupils making (a) 75 per cent of possible attendances the rate was £35 a year per pupil and £25 for day pupils. (b) 50 per cent of possible attendances £26.15 a year (boarding) and day £19.5 a year (c) 25 per cent of possible attendances and over, £17.10 a year. (boarding), £12.10 a year (day) (d) 10 per cent £8.15 a year (boarding); £12.10 a year. So, to get maximum grant-in-aid enforcement of pupil attendance was crucial. Incidentally, Alliance High School with, 85 pupils in 1931, got £2368 13 shs 37 cts.

Third, the rules required and thus imposed control on school expenditure, the governing board of every secondary school for Kenyans receiving aid was ordered to keep accounts as the director prescribed and to submit such accounts properly audited not later than the 23rd day of January of the year following the year grant was obtained.

Fourth, every secondary school aided by government in accordance with the rules, was required to be open to inspection by an education officer at any time.

The 1931 Education Ordinance further empowered the governor to make rules concerning the issue of teachers certificates in schools for Arabs and for Africans. Three grades of certificates were issuable commencing in 1932: Primary Certificate, Lower Primary Certificate, Elementary Certificate. The rules laid down a requirement to pass prescribed examinations in certain subjects and serving a one-year probationary period and evidence of good character satisfactory to the director before a certificate could be awarded. The rules were silent on the rate for remuneration.

The District Education Board Ordinance, 1934

This important ordinance set up district education boards to function in various parts of the country, with the district commissioner as chairman (ex-officio), the inspector of schools as secretary, a medical officer, an agricultural officer, representatives of missions and Africans nominated by local native councils, the boards exercised the following responsibilities:

> They were concerned with sub-elementary and elementary Education. Primary and secondary education was outside their jurisdiction. In connection with this responsibility the boards handled:

(a) allocation of grants subject to the approval of the director of education and the source of revenue being:

(i) grants from central funds and,

(ii) grants from local native councils.

(b) implementation of approved salary scales.

(c) matters to do with fees and scholarships.

(d) leasing of plots of land for school development.

(e) maintenance of a register of schools.

The boards generally were of value in controlling and financing elementary Education and quite often it was not necessary for the director of education to question their suggestions and decisions. By 1938, Kenya had three Education ordinances, two of which have by virtue of their important provisions been already written about, plus 16 rules relating to a number of subjects among which was school discipline. The operators of the schools were bound to observe the provisions of the ordinances and the rules, and the administrators of the Education system to see to their implementation and observance. Since education is a consumption good or service, always on demand, rules are necessary to ensure fair play.

Main stages of Kenyan African School System on the Eve of the Second World War (1939)

There were:
1. Sub-elementary schools – usually unaided, run by missions, manned by untrained and poorly paid teachers. Elements of Christian religion were taught plus Writing, Arithmetic, Hygiene, Drill and Gardening. Very few of them ever got a grant, but they taught more than half of Kenya's African children who could read.
2. Elementary schools. These offered a five-year elementary course based on a prescribed syllabus. The medium of instruction was the vernacular. English was taught as a subject in the last two forms. The elementary schools attempted to provide facilities for practical work.
3. Primary Schools. These were mainly boarding schools. However, a small number admitted day pupils. According to the annual report of the education department 1938 all approved primary schools had European principals assisted by one or more Europeans. They offered a three-year course in standard 6, 7 and 8 in literary and practical subjects. The medium of instruction was Kiswahili, but English could be used if permission was obtained from the director of education. The end of the course was marked by the Primary School Examination at which pupils were required to get a pass in one practical subject, Mathematics, one language and any other fourth subject. A certain degree of specialisation was allowed in that, a practically inclined pupil could be given more time in the practical subjects and less in the literary subjects and could obtain the Primary Certificate – if he passed Maths, Kiswahili, Agriculture and Crafts. A girl likewise could obtain the certificate in question with a pass in Arithmetic, Kiswahili and domestic Science. For secondary education, post officer and railway, a full ordinary course was necessary.
4. Girls' Boarding Schools. Under the care of the missions, these schools were grant aided and headed by a European courses were conducted related to the stage of education which girls had reached prior to their registration at the schools.

5. Secondary Schools. Secondary school development was painfully slow in colonial days and compared poorly with secondary school development in Uganda, for instance. Alliance High School, which was founded in 1926, for a considerable length of time, served all Protestant missions in Kenya regarding secondary education for African boys. About the same time the Roman Catholics established Kabaa as a secondary school. Secondary school development was not taken seriously until after the recommendations of the De La Warr Commission on higher education in East Africa of 1937.

The recommendations of the commission are stated and discussed fully in a later chapter in this book. What we would like to state here is that as a result of the commission's report, Kenya began to raise several of its upper primary schools, then known as high schools, to secondary school status. Hence Maseno and Yala in Nyanza and several others began their upward development.

When the development of secondary schools began to be accepted as a policy, the government policy for making agricultural and industrial education predominant in Kenya education for Africans stepped down into second place. A literary education which would lead to sitting for the Overseas Cambridge School Certificate Examination and eventually get into Makerere College became the aim of nearly all boys attending school. Failure to achieve this aim due to lack of financial support, or inability to pass examinations adequately well or due to some unpredictable circumstances, often caused painful frustration to pupils and parents. With getting into Makerere as the aim, the Kenyan secondary school pupil was reputed for being very hard-working and most enterprising. When he couldn't get a place in a Kenya secondary school he looked for an opportunity in one of Uganda's private secondary schools.

In 1939, Kenya had four secondary schools: Alliance High School, with 106 pupils, Kabaa High School (50 pupils), C.M.S. Maseno (58 pupils), and R. C. Yala, (17 pupils). Makerere College, which was then offering a secondary education course had 55 Kenyans whose fees were paid by Kenya's education department. These young men, like others from Uganda and Tanganyika, after two years of general education branched into teacher training, which the college offered.

6. Teacher training colleges. Lower primary teachers were trained in five centres, three of which were run by Catholic missions and two run by Protestants missions but inter-denominational Makerere College provided upper primary teachers.

7. Vocational schools. They accepted pupils who had completed standard VI. They included the health school and the Railway School, which catered for other parts of East Africa as well.

3

Education in the War Period 1939-1945

The Problems of War

The Second World War caused many problems in the development and administration of education in Kenya. First of all, its outbreak occasioned the departure of many missionaries from Kenya back to Britain and to other European countries so as to be available for active service as circumstances necessitated. Also missionaries who were expected to come to Kenya were unable to do so as they were expected for war activities at home. Moreover, enemy activities made travel dangerous, difficult and hazardous. Aeroplanes and ships were all open to attack by the enemy. There was a shortage of White people, who had been responsible for the running of education and indeed considered themselves as the only ones able to do so, and not the qualified Africans, whose number was very much limited then.

The scarcity of both resulted in a slow development in teacher education and secondary education. This was rather unfortunate because this was the time when it had been planned to make much effort for the development of secondary education in the whole of East Africa in order to get students to Makerere College, the college of higher learning for all East Africa, who would help in the meeting of the demand of manpower of a relatively higher academic standing.

Secondly, the war front attracted a lot of African men in Kenya. African teachers, who were numerous at this time in primary schools, were also affected by the desire to serve in the war, more especially because the salary offered there was far higher than that offered in the teaching service. There was quite a high demand for these teachers in the Seventh Battalion, to which all recruits from East and Central Africa belonged, for they could easily teach the many semi-literate men who were joining the war in their thousands. Thus a large number of male primary school teachers were enrolled in the Seventh Battalion. Reporting on this situation, the director of education in 1942 said:

> The demand by the Military Authorities for Africans who could read and write was as great in 1942 as in the previous war years and the number of boys who left Mission and Government schools before completing their courses was considerable. The high rate of pay offered in the army also drew away from schools some of the Elementary African Teachers. [7]

The Expansion of Primary Education

While the teaching force, especially in the primary schools, was decreasing the war period saw an increasing number of school children coming forward to attend primary schools. This was as a result of especially two factors. One was the rise in the earnings of the people of Kenya, especially those who were in a position to transport their crops to Nairobi. As the training camps for army recruits from all over East Africa, Malawi and Zambia, were based near Nairobi, one at Embakasi and the other at Kabete, there was a big demand for food by the government to feed the troops. Also these recruits used to get out of the camps, as all soldiers do, and buy such foodstuffs, as they required for themselves and for their friends.

Secondly, the large number of servicemen, which was reckoned to be one third of the adult male population of Kenya, got a wide experience out of their travels to Ethiopia, Far East and the Middle East. They realized that the traditional high respect which East Africans had given to the Europeans and Asians was not much in evidence in these places. Some of them felt that education had done much to emancipate those people, for they were doing similar skilled work and serving in skilled jobs similar in many respects to those of Europeans and Asians. Thus many Kenyans realised that the best salvation for their children was to give them a good school education. They could then match the European settlers and the Asians in knowledge and skill. Since all these servicemen had made good savings as a result of their war gratuities, they could easily send their children to school and those of their relatives as part of the extended families custom. The result of rising opportunities for farmers to sell their produce at good prices and the substantial savings from the war gratuities gave rise to school attendance of Kenya's children in big numbers. Rising attendance continued up to independence in 1963, and this is a characteristic of a developing education system that does not cater for everybody. Numbers are expected to rise every year very sharply, until nearly every child is brought under the ambit of the educational system.

The Problem of Financing the Expansion of Primary Education by Local Native Councils

The great increase in enrolment of pupils called for increases in the number of teachers, school buildings and other infrastructure. According to the 1934 grants-in-aid rules, rural primary schools were the responsibility of local native councils as far as finance was concerned. There were primary schools run by the missionaries and those run directly by the local native councils. The latter increased very much in number during the period under review. The local native councils financed all primary schools while the government met the costs for secondary, technical and teachers' schools and also the cost of all European education. But as the number of primary schools under the councils increased, the council's revenue through taxes tended to decrease, partly due to too many taxpayers having gone to the war front.

The local councillors were faced with a very big problem of running these schools on diminished funds. The children of their fellow Africans were demanding school education, which also the African councillors knew were the salvation of the Africans, yet they were faced with diminishing funds in relation to an expanding school system. So, rather than frustrate the parents and the children, the Local native councils chose to spend the greater part of their public funds on education and less on their social services. They soon got complaints from the central government, which took the view that there was an indiscriminate dishing out of grants-in-aid by the local native councils. These grants-in-aid should be concentrated specially on selected primary schools after ascertaining that they had reached as high a standard of efficiency as possible, and where the payment was intended to cover one half of the certified non-recurrent expenditure on buildings and equipment.

Unfortunately the African councillors had departed from this convention. They argued that this system allowed only a few people to benefit from public funds, thus depending on the proximity of parents' homes to a grant-aided school. The result was that any primary school that was opened was automatically given a small grant on buildings and equipment also to pay some teachers' salaries.

The Central Government's Failure to stop the Expansion of Primary Education

As a result of the central government's dissatisfaction with the manner in which the native councils gave out grants to primary schools it called for a revision of the grants-in –aid system in 1942. It was meant to curb the spending of money on primary schools by the local native councils at the expense of other social services. The government ordered that if a new school was built it should not be put on the list of those already on the grants-in-aid systems. The councils could keep only that number already on the grants-in-aids list. This ban dissatisfied the African members of these councils who demanded the control of the education system so as to expand it as they saw fit, and so save it from being squeezed by the pro-settler government. But this was not granted to them. To go round this ban the local native councils double-streamed those primary schools already on the list of grants-in-aid, and so the cost of education continued to soar just as before.

Unfortunately, the Colonial Government did not understand the force behind this expansion of primary schools, nor was it sympathetic to it, for it meant many burdens to it to provide funds for the ever-increasing African primary schools, which these councils could not meet. It also meant that if the local native councils spent most of their funds on education, the central government would be called upon to provide some money to keep the service running.

Meanwhile the settlers, taking advantage of the pre-occupation of the British government with the War, secured for themselves virtually "ministerial" positions in the government of Kenya. The Ministry of Education was given a hard-core settler whose European supporters were determined to see that the Africans had to be kept in "their proper place", that is to be given as few social amenities as possible while the Whites got as much as possible. So, the aspirations of the African Councillors for more primary schools met with no support from the pro-settler government. Even the Beecher Report of 1949 which was described as very sympathetic to the African educational aspirations, showed in effect the same attitude when it said:

It will be seen from this summary that there is a constant tendency for local enthusiasm to outstrip both financial provision and the long-term planning based on that provision. Thus there are always more schools being built than can be financed under the grants-in-aid rules; there are always fewer trained teachers than the system requires in order to be efficient.

The expansion at the bottom has been allowed to exceed the limits imposed by educational planning. In these conditions, everything expands except control, pressures result in all available money going into the provision of more visible schooling, without reference to quality, which depends on control and planning. The all-important provision of Secondary Education, which has remained within the limits imposed by the plan, is consequently of such a dimension as to be wholly inadequate in relation to the expansion of the primary system. So the bottom of the system cannot be enlarged until the bottom has been improved. [8]

It should be noted that the pro-settler government was responsible for the secondary schools and therefore it was responsible for the lack of expansion. Notwithstanding Beecher's remarks quoted above, local native councils continued to aid the struggling primary schools. To the Kenyans, the government stand looked quite unfair, since by 1942 the Europeans and Asian children had Universal Primary Education which the government, to a very large extent, financed in such a way that it built most luxurious primary schools for these two communities, especially the European community.

The Question of the Supply of Teachers and their Salaries

While the opening up of more schools was going on there was the question of the supply of teachers. Many qualified primary teachers had gone to the war front. The output of the teachers' colleges did not keep in step with the rapid opening up of schools, because most funds were devoted to the war effort, and so it was not possible to increase the number of such institutions, more especially as the central government kept a controlling hand on them. The primary schools were left with no other alternative but to engage unqualified men and women to teach in them. So many unqualified teachers entered Kenya primary schools to keep the African education system running for their fellow Africans, and much was owed to those men and women for the maintenance of the system.

Local native councils were in great difficulties over the payment of these teachers, qualified and unqualified at the same time trying to provide for other social services. The central government worsened the situation when it decided to raise the salaries of teachers in primary schools it maintained, to meet the raising cost of living. Local native councils could not increase the salaries of their teachers. There arose, therefore, a disparity in salary between teachers working in government schools and those in local native council schools. Inevitably, employees in local council schools registered dissatisfaction. However, Kenyans were not discouraged in their efforts to expand primary education.

4

The Era of the Beecher Ten-Year Development Plan 1949-1963

Introduction 1945-1949

After the war, Kenyans justifiably felt that the central government was not doing enough to provide enough schools at all levels for the Africans. The European and Asian communities had since 1942 had more or less enough schools, and more were being built for them every year as the need arose, and they had compulsory primary education up to the age of 15. For Africans, development was painfully slow, perhaps because of their large numbers but mainly because of a wrong philosophy, which the colonialists decided to use as a guide to the development of education for Kenyan Africans.

The philosophy had two strands. The first was that the African should be given what is considered appropriate. After all, they were not being educated to play the same role as that of Europeans and Asians. The Europeans were being educated to be leaders and the Asians to be commercial and industrial magnets, while the Africans were employed to serve both by doing jobs that were below their dignity of the two groups.

The second strand was that, economically the Africans as individuals contributed far less financially to the government coffers than the Europeans and Asians. So what they got out of the system needed to be commensurate with what they put in. Viewed broadly, the philosophy was most unacceptable and it meant stagnation rather than effective development of the educational facilities for the Africans. Financially, the Africans were individually bound to contribute less, because the colonial system was such that the low paying jobs were the ones reserved for them, and there was no way of getting out of this because their education was kept deliberately low, thus rendering them ineligible for higher and better paid jobs. There were few jobs where Africans could be in position of authority, since many jobs were normally thought to be the preserve of Europeans or Asians.

Worse still, most of their best land had been taken away from them and given to the colonial settlers. So, even through agriculture, they could not hope to make much money. How then could Africans as individuals contribute as much tax as the Europeans and the Asians? But taken collectively, their financial contribution could not be ignored and this should have justified provision of more facilities for their education.

The dissatisfaction expressed by the Africans regarding the kind of education and the educational facilities they were being given, led to several commissions being set up in 1945, 1946 and 1948, each of which was charged with the duty of framing a plan of education for the Africans that would satisfy them. All the plans produced by these commissions, however, dominated by government officials and missionaries many of whom could be influenced by settlers' sentiments, were disallowed by the Advisory Council on African Education as not going far enough to help the Africans.

The Beecher Committee of 1949

Finally, in 1949 a committee headed by Archdeacon Beecher, a missionary who was a great sympathiser of the Africans, was set up to use all the previous commissions' reports and work out a more agreeable ten-year plan for the development of African education. Government accepted the plan and it was adopted in 1950. It was on the basis of this Beecher Education Committee's work that Kenya's education developed up to independence in 1963. The plan was based on the needs of each district, which happened to vary throughout the country. The intention was that a more advanced district should not be retarded in its educational development by the relatively greater needs, and necessarily slower progress, of a more slow moving neighbour. So the Beecher plan composed plans for each district so that each district could advance at its own pace. The district could even raise fees or charge an educational tax depending on the financial ability of the people within that particular district. The Beecher plan was a 4-4-4 system.

It was designed to give four years of primary education to 50 per cent of the children of school age within ten years. This was supposed to ensure that there would be sufficient pupils going on to teaching and to secondary schools ending up with a School Certificate. It provided for only 30 per cent of pupils completing primary four to proceed to the next stage called the intermediate, again lasting for four years. Only the children of Nairobi and Mombasa were supposed to have the full range of the primary education of eight years because in these two places there were enough facilities and teachers to manage the work.

It was especially the provision that only 30 per cent would proceed to the intermediate stage, that made the majority of the people in Kenya oppose the plan very bitterly. Kenyans contended that 30 per cent was too small a number of children to complete primary education. Taking into account drop-outs, which were was inevitable at this rate, only a very small number would continue to secondary school. The majority of Kenyan people never supported the Beecher recommendations wholeheartedly.

Education after the Beecher Plan had been Accepted

During the decade after the Beecher plan had been accepted, enrolment of primary pupils rose from one third to four-fifths of a million. For example, between 1955 and 1960, enrolment for the intermediate section rose from 7,600 to 156,000 pupils. This went beyond the stipulated numbers to be accommodated by the plan, and it showed the determination of the Kenyan people to send their children to school despite the limitation imposed by the plan, and the local native councils worked hard to set up primary schools. But more than 80 per cent of these pupils were in the first four years of primary schools, and the girls were relatively few.

The Problem of Wastage

The situation where the first four years had many more of the pupils than the four years of the upper primary and the four years of the secondary section, could be explained as a result of tremendous wastage that was a general feature of East African education during the colonial period. There were several causes for this in the case of Kenya. Examinations at frequent intervals caused the termination of schooling of many pupils. There was a public examination at the end of the first four years of primary, there was another one after primary eight known as the Kenya African Preliminary Examination, then another one at the end of the tenth year called the Kenya African Secondary Examination, followed by the Cambridge School Certificate Examination at the end of the twelfth year.

Before the Makerere Entrance Examination was abolished in 1948, there was also this examination in the twelfth year. Each of these examinations was supposed to mark the end of an academic section and to give the African child a sense of achievement, so that if he stopped there he would have a certificate which he would use as a qualification for employment, or if not for getting a job, at least to show that he had attended school. These examinations also were used to select pupils for the next stages, which always had limited places. Those administering the system had only a limited number of places to offer in the next section, so that they fixed a fairly high pass mark.

The question of school fees too, caused wastage. It even prevented pupils from finishing one of the stages within the education system. Then there were other reasons such as waywardness of some pupils, something peculiar to children the world over. There was also the feeling of some pupils after years of study that they had enough, even if a stage had not been completed. After all, though educationists may feel that for a pupil to gain anything out of a stage in an educational system, needs to complete it, this is not obvious to the pupil who may feel that he has had enough even before the end of such a stage. This was common during the 1940s and 1950s in East Africa when pupils attending primary schools were relatively older than today, and thus they could easily judge that they had got what they wanted out of attending school at any point in the stage at which they were. Then there were also the pupils who were excluded because of the scarcity of places especially at the end of primary four, for not all who passed the above examination could be accommodated in the next stage as vacancies were very few. Pupils in this category, especially used to experience much frustration. This is one reason why Uganda's independent private schools at secondary level were so much sought after by pupils coming from Kenya. Those who had completed primary four and primary eight and failed to get places in Kenyan intermediate and secondary schools would proceed to Uganda to seek education in private schools. Both groups used to get enrolled in the secondary section, although the former in normal cases would not qualify for secondary education. But because the proprietors of these schools did not know the Kenyan system of education and, because they wanted money, they just enrolled anybody who presented himself.

The economic commission that visited Kenya from 1953 to 1955 observed the serious shortage of school places, and also commented on the great wastage as a result of examinations. They wrote:

> ...perhaps the most important stage of all educational problems for the East African governments to tackle is the elimination of wastage. The grading of classes and schools proceed on the assumption that, of the pupils who enter the primary schools at an average of about seven years, half will for one reason or another, have dropped out by the time the end of the primary course is reached. Four fifths of those who remain will then be eliminated by examination and for only half of the remainder places will be found in intermediate schools. Of these, a further 80 per cent will either leave during the intermediate course or be eliminated at the end of it. In other words, out of every one hundred children entering primary schools, only ten will be able to find places in intermediate school that is from primary five to primary eight. And of those who go through the secondary schools, only a small proportion is at the end of it able to pass the school certificate examination. This evolves a shocking wastage of money and effort and is responsible for the creation of a difficult social problem. [9]

Secondary Education for Kenyans Developed Painfully Slowly

The Education Report of 1955 showed that 31.2 per cent of pupils were completing the first four years of primary and 3.7 per cent were completing the eighth year, while 0.08 per cent were completing the twelfth class and sitting for the School Certificate Examination. Even as the end of this period approached the secondary section had a very small intake, which was as follows: 1958: 13 per cent, 1959: 12 per cent and 1960: 12.5 per cent. This was indeed too small a number in face of the high demand for manpower needs at secondary level, especially with the approach of independence. Towards 1960, efforts were made to reduce wastage at primary and intermediate levels which resulted in an increasing number of boys and girls being enrolled for secondary courses. These were so many that the gradual development recommended by the Beecher Report had been superseded by 1963. Each district got a number of highly organised secondary schools numbering 41 in the whole country by 1960. The reasons for the disappointingly small intakes at secondary schools were shown in the report of the economic commission already quoted. This development in secondary education was reflected in the number of students joining Makerere.

5

Agriculture and Technical Education

(i) Agricultural Education

Time and again some people have complained that during the colonial period the subject of Agriculture was given a minor place compared to the academic subjects. However, records show that there was a determined effort to teach Agriculture and also those students who attended these courses are present to testify to the reality of this. If the graduates of these schools have had less effect on our society in putting what they learnt into practice, that is a different matter.

The aim of the primary schools in Kenya was to teach the children basic subjects such as Arithmetic and Reading, and to encourage manual dexterity and elementary self-discipline among them.

In intermediate schools, that is from Primary Five to Primary Eight, pupils were given lessons in Handicrafts, Home Crafts and in Agriculture. Thus the Director of Education in 1951 said:

> The intermediate school prepares its pupils on the one hand for further education, on the other its curriculum is so planned that its emphasis on practical work, on home crafts and on agriculture will produce young men and women who can play a full part in the economic and social life of the community. The policy is to make it available for each African child to show its importance.

> Until such time as there are sufficient intermediate schools to meet the needs of the children completing their primary school course, there will be the problem of the child who leaves school without the opportunity of further formal education. It is hoped also that many intermediate schools will serve as community centres and thus provide the opportunity for the starting of schemes for informal education for both boys and girls who return to their homes after leaving the primary schools. [10]

The Rural Training Centre at Thogoto took on T.3 teachers, who were given an additional year in Agriculture and got a certificate, to help pupils become interested in this subject. Teachers of Handicraft were trained at the Government African School at Embu, but the course was transferred to Kagumo Teacher Training Centre in 1953. At Egerton Agricultural College one got a Diploma in Agriculture after two years' training after secondary education. Smallholdings were attached to intermediate schools with the very full co-operation of the agricultural department.

Also at Egerton, short courses for farmers were held. Hence the education report of 1951 said:

> Schools have been regularly visited by agricultural officers and agricultural inspectors. Particular attention was devoted in the central province to demonstration of manure and compost preparation, fodder growing, bench terracing and rotation of crops and grass. Arrangements were made for parties of parents to attend these demonstrations. In Nyeri District, 25 farmers' clubs have been formed. [11]

There were also other agricultural schools in Kenya, which gave lessons to adults, such as Ukara Farm Institute in Nyanza. Such schools took several families for a year. Each one lived on its own holding or a group farm run on grass and plough rotation. At such schools also, refresher courses covering crop rotation and the principles of mixed farming were held for agricultural instructors, teachers and farmers. Officers and senior instructors of the agricultural department, adopted schools in which they demonstrated recommended local agricultural practices.

In 1947 when an agricultural education officer to the Nyanza Province was appointed he reported:

> In primary schools the old-fashioned school garden is giving place to a series of small demonstration and experimental plots which are in effect the outside laboratory, which serves for instruction both in agriculture and nature study, the aim being that pupils should learn to link up cause and effect and to make use of that knowledge. [12]

His colleague in the Central Province wrote:

> The old idea that education has to do with books rather than with hoes is undoubtedly going, but the hammer has not yet finally fallen. It is safe to say that all schools are soil-conscious and that conservation practice has a deservedly large place in the teaching; many secondary schools have under taken an ambitious fencing programme and have good paddocks for rational grazing and schools are recognising that improved conditions must precede improved stock. Regular dipping or spraying is the next step. [13]

Attempts to set up primary schools in the 1940s, with a bias towards the occupations of the people in the area in question must not be forgotten. For example, at the Government Primary School of Kabianga, which served the pastoral tribe of Kipsigis, a primary course with a strong veterinary bias was introduced. A similar school was set up in Maasai at the government African School of Narok. Another one was set up Baringo.

The policy of interesting intermediate pupils in agriculture was pursued because they were older, and were supposed to be a middle class group on graduation who could influence the rural areas by their numbers and example. Efforts were made by officers from the agriculture department to arrange agricultural projects in the neighbourhood of intermediate schools, seeking to secure the interests of the pupils of those schools in such projects. There were also plans to arrange agricultural training camps for those that had left or were about to leave intermediate schools. The Beecher Report of 1949 recommended relating the intermediate syllabus to agricultural problems.

Emphasis on agriculture in intermediate schools was indicated in 1950 education department report which said:

> The intermediate schools prepares its pupils on the one hand for further education, on the other its curriculum is so framed that its emphasis on practical work, on home craft and on agriculture will produce young men and women who can play a full part in the economic and social life of the community.[14]

It was also envisaged that many intermediate schools would serve as community centres and thus provide the opportunity for starting schemes for informal education for both boys and girls who returned to their homes after leaving primary schools. But it was never practised and it remained on paper. East Africa's educational development has numerous examples of this kind where the good idea never got off the ground.

(ii) Technical Education

As seen in previous chapters, from the beginning of school education in Kenya the system emphasized the technical side of education and the Fraser recommendations of 1909 which laid down the basis of education to be given to the different races of Kenya, were that Africans should be given mainly industrial and agricultural education. As a result, the government opened up an industrial school at Machakos in 1915 and the Native Industrial Training Depot at Kabete in 1924, where training was directed towards the production of artisans for the building trades. In 1930 the government embarked on a programme of building a considerable number of African schools, and it was decided that students of the above schools should carry this out. Consequently, many secondary schools such as Machakos, Kagumo, Kisii, Shimo-la-Tewa and Kakamega were built by teams of students form Kabete.

The Technical School of Kabete was handed over to the army during the Second World War and after the war up to 1948, it continued to be used to rehabilitate ex-servicemen, giving them courses to enable them put to use many of the skills they had got as a result of war training. Thus the department of education annual report for 1950 said:

> The war had interrupted the training and education of members of young Kenya men and women at an age when they would normally be taking courses of further education or training for a business or professional career. On the other hand, many persons while engaged in the war service have been enabled to obtain valuable vocational training and experience. The Kenya Government recognized the

importance of securing to the country, after the war, the service and influence of these persons, whether European, Asian or African.[15]

Kabete was handed back to the department of education in 1948 to continue as a technical and trade school. Other trade and technical schools, which were set up during the period under review, were Thika Technical and Trade school, Nyanza Technical and Trade School at Sigalala, and Kwale Technical and Trade School in the Coast Province. All these, and the ones that were set up before this period, taught carpentry and building, painting, plumbing and pipe fitting, blacksmithing and welding, shoe-making and leather working, tailoring, fitting and general garage work.

In 1949 the building of the Mombasa Institute of Moslem Education started. The purpose of the institute was to provide technical and trade education for Moslems from all parts of East Africa. The institute started to take in students in 1951.

Early in 1950s the Willoughby Committee recommended the opening up of a technical school giving higher courses than the ones provided in trade and technical schools. Subsequently the Royal Technical College was built in Nairobi and it opened its doors to students in 1956. While it was being built, Dr. F. G. Harlow, Assistant Education Advisor for Technical Education to the Colonial Office, advised the introduction of technical and commercial courses in secondary schools, which would prepare pupils for the opportunities which the Royal Technical College would offer, and his advice was followed.

This period saw great enthusiasm for technical education, especially as the expanding industries of Nairobi were looking for qualified manpower and people saw opportunities of good employment in store. In the field of trade training the number of applications received from African boys seeking admission to these trade schools was rising sharply, and it was matched by an increasing demand from industry for trained artisans, particularly in the engineering trades.

The minimum entry qualifications were intermediate education. Later at Kabete they were raised to Secondary Two, and by 1955 the school certificate that required. By 1960 enrolment in the five trade schools of Machakos, Kabete, Singala, Kwale and Thika was 1128 students.

Two new Asian secondary schools were given a technical and commercial bias, and began to function as technical high schools in 1959. In the same year, the Nairobi Technical Institute was built after plans had been discussed for it 15 years earlier. It was later named the Kenya Polytechnic. It opened its doors in 1961. It offered courses leading to the City and Guilds of London Institute and the Union of Lancashire and Cheshire Institutes examinations.

From 1952 the labour department introduced a system of trade testing. It conducted courses similar to those in the trade schools while it provided fairly competent knowledge in each trade to the students who enrolled for the courses.

From the very beginning of trade school system, the training included a considerable amount of productive work at all schools. Material produced was sold or used in the schools, and indeed they showed their worth in this way by contributing to the economy of the country. An interesting side to this was the follow-up given to graduates from the trade and technical schools by their instructors, to see how they progressed. All boys leaving these schools were placed in employment without difficulty because there was a great demand for them in industry.

In 1957 an experiment was made to enable technical school leavers to start businesses for their own. These formed building teams of between five and ten people who had finished the training. They were given a loan from the International Co-operation Administration, plus essential equipment and tools to enable them operate a small contracting company. Employment was found for the team within the school building programme, and with the supervision of instructors from the trade school they carried out sufficient building work to pay off the loans within 18 months. The success of this experiment warranted the expansion of the scheme. By 1960 over 20 such schemes had been established.

6

Racialism in Education and Inequality in Facilities for Education

Racialism

As described earlier, from the very time the Kenya colonial government started to concern itself with education in 1911, by setting up a department of Education, it made it clear that education had to be run along racial lines. That is, each group of children had to attend different schools and also get different instructions. Consequently, European children had their own schools, Asian children had theirs, which again were subdivided according to the Asian castes, and the Arabs had theirs; at the bottom of the ladder came schools for Africans. Some of these were under different Christian denominations, others were under the local native Councils, though all African schools were given the same treatment.

Perhaps in a colonial situation this kind of educational arrangement could not be avoided, where the white settlers and other Whites felt superior to the Asians and Africans and where a situation was created that Asians and Arabs looked at themselves as being superior to the Africans; and where it was believed that each group of people had a different role to play and a different status to conserve which were peculiar to its ethnicity. In fact all over East Africa education was characterised by this racial segregation, but it was more pronounced in Kenya because the country had more Europeans, who they looked at Kenya as their own country, where they had come to stay for good, and where the interests of the Whites were taken to be paramount. Europeans in the rest of East Africa, who were mostly civil servants, used to send their children to Kenyan schools for education, except temporarily during the Second World War, when the European schools in Kenya could not cope with the number of children from all over Central and East Africa, for the building programme of their schools was rather retarded by the scarcity of funds due to the war.

Segregation in education on racial lines, bred serious social attitudes in Kenya among people who were living in one political area. And this is a glaring example of how man can deliberately create social classes in a country which becomes obsessed with their special places and privileges.

Inequality in Education facilities

Primary education for European children was compulsory from 1909. This also began to apply to the Asian children from 1942. European schools were heavily subsidised by government and partly aided by Asian communal self-help, which arose from the great benefits which they were reaping from trade and industry. In terms of what was spent on European education, in comparison to African education, one sees that the European education, which was for fewer children, took a much larger portion of government expenditure as the statistics show. Luxurious primary and secondary schools were built for Whites and were maintained at a very high standard, while the African schools of the same level were left poor in buildings and services. The philosophy here was that of appropriateness. It was argued with conviction that the European children had standards already established, and these had to be maintained in schools, while the Africans had no similar standards in amenities at home, and anything was good for them however it was. A philosophy of this nature would have left no room for the improvement of the Africans, as everything that was better than what they had before was considered as inappropriate.

The second point in this trend of thought was, as already mentioned, that the community which paid higher taxes as per individual should be given greater social amenities by government.

The government's education policy during this period underlined these points. For example, while every European child was entitled to universal primary education, and provisions were made to see that there were enough schools to effect this, the rising demand for primary education on the African side received token response. The colonial government even curbed the enthusiasm of the local native councils to set up enough schools for the African children, calling this over-hasty on the part of these councils.

European children were assured of secondary school education, which also included the top two classes for Higher School Certificate. Once they completed this they were helped by government to continue to higher education institutions or, on occasion, to get good employment. Reporting proceedings of the Conference of Education in East Africa of 1946, the Kenya department of education said:

> The conference resolved to recommend to the East African Governments that European boys leaving Secondary Schools in East Africa and unable to secure immediate employment or higher training, to go to the U.K. for military service. Such service should enable them to qualify for admission to institutions of higher or vocational education in the U.K. on the same terms as U.K. candidates who have also completed their military serve.[16]

The system of education for the European and for the Africans was drastically different. The African system was divided into several parts, as we have seen, the primary section covering the first four years ending with an examination, the intermediate section covering four years at the end of which pupils did the Kenya African Preliminary Examination; the secondary section was divided again into two parts, the first one lasting for two years. After the first part the African pupil sat for examination called the Kenya African Secondary, the result of which either allowed him to proceed to the last two classes and finally sit for the Cambridge School Certificate Examination, or made him look for a job or go for a professional training. But the European children and the Asians did not have this kind of arrangement.

They had a primary education lasting for six years, and a secondary education lasting for eight years, with only three examinations in the whole system. The Asian children followed more or less a similar system to that of the Europeans, although at the end of the primary education they sat for an examination called the Kenya Asian Primary Examination, while the European children sat for the Kenya European Primary Examination. It was only from 1960 that all the races started to sit for the same Primary Leaving Examination. This was after political pressure was exerted urging all races to pull together in the spirit of *harambee*. But during the days when it looked as if the White man would be the sole master of Kenya, it could never be thought feasible to bring the three systems of education together. It was at Makerere College that some sort of coming together of the three races was envisaged from 1953, where also amenities similar to those in Kenyan, European and Asian schools could not be found. Yet the majority of European and Asian students tended to go to Southern Rhodesia, South Africa and the United Kingdom. The Kenya colonial government gave them scholarships and bursaries to study in those countries. Both European and Asian education at primary and secondary level developed very much during this period and it gave an impetus to the Africans to aspire so high in order to vie with these two groups of people.

The Arabs too tended to follow their own education system. At primary school level the Arab children generally attended their own schools and tended to join the Asian secondary schools. As a result, they too, had better educational facilities than Africans.

Kenyans were reasonably feeling uneasy about the great disparity of educational facilities between the European and Asian communities on one side and the African community on the other. But the feeling seems to have made no impression on the colonial government which had its own ideas regarding the development of education for Kenyans. The Beecher Report indicated this in the most unacceptable remarks it made in 1949. The report said:

> African education in relation to African society cannot be compared with education in European and Asian society. No purpose is served by using any comparison as the basis of financial provision. The time has not yet come when African education

can be put together with European and Asian educational services and a given sum of money allocated to each on the basis of any statistical or other formula. European and Asian education each have a much longer history, both races have in varying degrees achieved high standards in the preliminary objectives of literacy and have already recognized standards by which they assess economically purposeful educational results. The peculiar nature of African education, with its limited achievement, and long range of objectives, is such that long term planning alone, and consequently long term financial provision are appropriate. We are only at the stage of establishing a means by which future results may be achieved; European and Asian educational system are concerned with maintaining long and well established standards.[17]

The White and Asian communities looked at African education as needing gradual development and for which money should be spent sparingly while an appreciably large amount of money spent on the education of European and Asian children was regarded justified. In conclusion, it is reasonable to suggest firmly that in Kenya's educational system there was a strong racial bias meant to create different societies within one political area.

During the Second World War the independent schools increased in number to help meet the high demand for primary education during this time, which could not be satisfied by the mission, government and local native councils. The movement soon spread from Kikuyu territory. After the war, independent schools were established in Kericho, Ukamba, Rift Valley and in Kisii District. A number of these developed into junior secondary schools. But before they reached the final stage of full secondary status, the majority of them, 184 in number, including the Kenya African Teachers College at Githunguri were proscribed by the colonial government in 1952 as one of the measures taken to check Kenya's great political revolution known otherwise as Mau Mau. The few that remained in Nyeri District were only saved because their manager, Johana Kunyih, handed them over to the district education board of Nyeri to be the responsibility of the local native council.

Independent schools were taken by the colonial administration to be political hot-beds of fanatical nationalism and propaganda dissemination against the colonial government. The director of education in 1952 had nothing good to say about them. Reporting in December the director said:

> Before and after the declaration of a state of Emergency it became obvious that many African independent schools had been used for spreading propaganda against the Government and for encouraging the growth of the Mau Mau Movement. In some cases teachers and members of the school committees had been sent to prison for subversive activities and for participation in Mau Mau ceremonies, sometimes all the children in a school had been forced to take the Mau Mau oath, sometimes the schools had been used for Mau Mau ceremonies. For this reason the Kikuyu Independent Schools Association and the Kikuyu Karinga Education Association were banned. Children from closed schools were told to join either Mission or Local Native Councils schools.[18]

This seems to have been an exaggerated statement because research has shown that the members of former independent schools did not dominate the Freedom fighters' struggle which the director referred to as Mau Mau.

It was unfortunate however that these schools were closed down at a time when they were moving into a position of offering secondary education while the demand for it was rising rapidly, and while the government and the mission secondary schools could not absorb even a third of this demand.

7

Teacher Education and Types of Teachers

By 1939 the education system was gradually becoming fully manned by African teachers at the primary school level and efforts were being made throughout this period to produce these teachers through numerous teacher training centres. The war , however, retarded the expansion of the institutions that were necessary to cope with the production of teachers for the ever-increasing numbers of pupils.

Students who entered a teacher training college after their primary eight education had a course lasting for two years, and they were classified into two groups. Those who had passed their Kenya African Preliminary Examination were classified as Grade II teachers or T.3, and those who had not passed it and yet had followed a similar teachers' course were classified as Grade III teachers or T.4. Both types of teachers taught in the first four classes of the primary section.

Men and women who sat for and passed the Kenya African Secondary School Examination and underwent training as teachers for two years, came out as assistant teachers Grade I and taught in the intermediate schools, Standard Five through Eight. Cambridge School Certificate holders trained for two years and were classified as Kenya Teachers Grade I (K.T.I) and taught the upper classes of the intermediate schools. There were not many of them.

At Thogoto Rural Training Centre there was a one-year course for Grade II teachers teaching Agriculture in the intermediate schools. If these teachers taught well, after two years they were promoted to assistant teachers Grade I. In 1953 a similar arrangement was made for handicraft teachers at the Government African School, Embu, and in 1956 the course was transferred to Kagumo Teacher Training College. All K.T.I. teachers trained at Kagumo and Siriba Government Teachers Centres. The rest of the teachers, except those of agriculture and handicraft, were trained at Makerere College, which until recently was the only institution for training secondary school teachers proper.

Teachers' Union Formed

During the period under review, teachers made efforts to organise themselves into a strong union to press for improvement of their conditions of service. This need tended to be felt more among teachers in the lower stages of the educational ladder. As was the case in Uganda, the question of who employed the teachers was still unsettled. Was it the central government or the various bodies that engaged them, such as the missions and the local native councils? The position, as it was then, was unsatisfactory. Each body which employed a group of teachers was their employer. But each employing body had its own conditions of service for the teachers it employed. Teachers engaged by the local governments had theirs and those engaged by missionary bodies had theirs too. Salary scales were different. For example in 1961, in one district alone, there were 12 Christian employment bodies, each of which gave different conditions of service to the teachers and even different salaries. Some teachers were civil servants, especially all European and Asian teachers in grant-aided schools and a few African teachers. The majority of African teachers, however, employees of local authorities and of various voluntary agencies, were not civil servants.

Civil servants had better conditions of service, were on a pension scheme and enjoyed housing allowance, medical attention, leave and travel allowance. For the non-civil servant teachers these benefits were out of the question, a fact which much lowered their morale.

There obviously was a need to have a unified teaching service with the same conditions of service for all teachers. Even among government teachers who were employed under the civil service terms, European and Asian teachers had a non-compulsory contributory scheme. Furthermore, the rules of conduct made for African teachers implied they were regarded as an irresponsible group of people who could hardly choose between good and bad. One monstrous rule, for instance, was that a male teacher should never be seen talking to a female teacher on the compound although they were on the same staff.

African teachers were justifiably much dissatisfied with the state of affairs and they began to organise themselves into a union in the early 1940s. This union was called the Kenya African Teachers' Union (KATU). But the union died soon after its formation, due to tribal, religious and other conflicts. Another attempt was made in 1952 and teachers from all over Kenya formed the Kenya African Teachers Organisation (KATO), but like many organisations then, it was banned as soon as a State of Emergency was declared.

In 1957 Daniel arap Moi, later President of Kenya, tabled a motion in the then Legislative Council that a teachers' organisation be formed. The motion was allowed and the government appointed B.A. Ohanga to organise the teachers. However, teachers from Nyanza objected to the appointment of Ohanga by the government on the grounds that teachers were capable of organising themselves. So in December 1957 teachers from all over Kenya sent representatives to Nairobi where they met and formed the present Kenya National Union of Teachers (KNUT).

Today Kenya has one of the best organised and strongest teachers' unions in Africa. It is very active and it has well equipped offices in every district with a permanent staff chosen from among the teachers themselves.

Notes

1. Cole Keith, *Kenya Hanging in the Middle Way Highway* Press London.
2. *Kenya Education Department Annual Report, 1931,* Government Printer, Nairobi.
3. *Native Affairs Annual Report, 1924,* Government Printer, Nairobi.
4. *Kenya Education Department Annual Report, 1926,* Government Printer, Nairobi.
5. *Native Affairs Annual Report, 1929.*
6. *Kenya Education Department Annual Report, 1937,* Government Printer, Nairobi.
7. *Kenya Education Department Annual Report, 1942,* Government Printer, Nairobi.
8. *A Ten-Year Plan for the Development of African Education,* Government Printer, Nairobi 1949.
9. *East African Royal Commission Report, 1951-1953.*
10. *Kenya Education Department Annual Report, 1951*
11. *Ibid.*
12. *Kenya Education Department Annual Report, 1947,* Government Printer, Nairobi, 1947.
13. *Ibid.*
14. *Kenya Education Department Annual Report, 1950,* Government Printer, Nairobi.
15. *Ibid*
16. *Kenya Education Department Annual Report, 1946.* Government Printer, Nairobi.
17. *Ten-Year Plan for the Development of African Education,* Government Printer, Nairobi, 1949.
18. *Kenya Education Department Annual Report, 1952,* Government Printer, Nairobi.

PART TWO

DEVELOPMENT OF EDUCATION IN UGANDA 1900-1962

8

Pioneer Work of the Missionaries 1900-1925

Despite the recurrent political and religious violence of the 1890s, problems involved in getting accepted by Ugandans, and their invidious rivalry, the Protestant and Catholic missions pioneered the task of starting and keeping going a school education system for many years with very little or no financial assistance from the government. Over the years, they had reached a position where they enjoyed so much influence over the protectorate government, the Ugandan traditional rulers of kingdoms and other integral administrative units of the country. This included a sway over the men who held the office of chief. With some assistance from external sources, plus the industry of their personnel, up to 1925 all school education was in the hands of the missions.

Except at Makerere where the protectorate government had put up a school to train mechanics and carpenters, and a few centres where medical workers were trained, all school buildings and teachers in the country belonged to the missionary groups. Their commitments were heavy and really testing. What objectives did missionaries wish to achieve? At first, their cardinal objective was to make their converts literate so that they could refresh their religious knowledge in their homes by reading the Bible and other simple books which the missions published and provided. However, by 1901 the missionaries, following the request by Catholic chiefs of Buganda kingdom, led by the leading Catholic Chief Stanislaus Mugwanya for a higher school that would mainly teach English, began to consider seriously the need for a form of education designed to help build the character of the pupils and to prepare them for a wider and fast changing world in which they would live. It was felt that this aim could best be achieved through a boarding high school education system using English as the medium of instruction.

The first school along such lines was started by Mill Hill Fathers in 1902 at Namilyango, 19 kilometres away from Kampala. The first carefully selected group of pupils, who were sons of Catholic chiefs were, in addition to being taught Reading, Writing, and Arithmetic also taught English Grammar, Geography, Mathematics, Music and Games. After Namilyango College, many other schools of similar type were opened up. Among these were Mengo High School 1903, Gayaza High School 1905, King's College Budo 1906, Kamuli, Kisubi (originally St. Mary's School, Rubaga 1906) Mbarara, and Bukalasa. The majority of those schools were mainly for the sons and daughters of more influential families who, it was assumed, would soon or later hold positions of responsibility as chiefs, for example.

Missionary Schools

By the year 1924 when the Phelps-Stokes Commission visited Uganda, missionaries operated six types of schools:

1. Colleges. There were three of these namely, King's College Budo, the top school of the Church Missionary School (CMS) education system and Namilyango College the apex of the Mill Hill Mission education system, and lastly Kisubi College, the apex of the White Fathers' mission education system. Although set up by different missionary groups, as indicated in the CMS Board of Education Scheme for Uganda in 1909, the colleges all alike aimed at producing morally, upright and honest Christian clerks, traders, interpreters and chiefs. The colleges were headed by men in Holy orders (priests), and stressed use of English as the medium of instruction.
2. Normal Schools. For training teachers

3. High Schools. Usually boarding and headed by a European with a high level of efficiency and education, maintained that English be taught to all classes, and of about the standard of Primary Seven or junior secondary. Examples of these were Mengo High School, Ngora High School, Hoima, Kabarole, Mbarara, Kamuli, Nabumali, Nandere, Kitovu, Nsambya and Gayaza for Protestant girls and Villa Maria for Catholic girls. All boys' high schools at best acted as preparatory schools for the three colleges Kisubi, Budo, and Namilyango. The girls high schools, on the other hand, regarded themselves as the apex of the girls' education. One of their chief objectives was to produce a girl accomplished, in all ways, for the requirements of a housewife in Uganda. Products of these schools, of course, today advanced in age, recall the long hours they spent digging, plaiting mats, cooking and sweeping the floor and some hold that their curriculum was so designed as to make them inferior to men educationally.
4. Central School. Day schools providing rudimentary education.
5. Sub-grade. Of uncertain educational value – no staff in any way qualified and no supervision.
6. Maternity schools. These trained midwives.

These mission educational institutions were mainly financed by the tuition fees mainly collected in central government and boarding schools, large grants from Diocesan funds raised by the members of the Church in question, and small grants from kingdoms and other local government units where feasible. Government aid was very little compared with the financial aid from these sources. The Phelps-Stokes Commission 1924, thus urged the government to step up considerably the grants to missions for educational work. It would be safe to say that generally speaking, missionaries had some sort of institution in the majority of the districts comprising Uganda. However, while they did their utmost to improve educational facilities, their overzealous approach to religion tended to make their institutions produce educated Roman Catholics or Protestants rather than educated Ugandans.

Furthermore, whether intended or not, they forced a break with some aspects of Ugandan home life and in many ways tried hard, and indeed succeeded, in insulating their pupils against Ugandan customary or traditional education. Indeed they seem to have operated on the false assumption that they brought education to absolutely uneducated Africans. There was, as we have already pointed out, and point out again , traditional education, and there is no doubt at all about it. In recent years African scholars have, at least, convinced the hardest of the doubters through research followed by thesis (for degrees), that traditional education existed in Uganda although literacy and formal schooling were not associated with it.

The Phelps-Stokes Commission 1924 Reports on Education in Uganda

In 1924 the trustees of the Phelps-Stokes Fund USA, a philanthropic foundation devoted to the education of Black Americans, Africans, and American Indians, with the participation of missionary societies in Britain and America, caused the African Educational Commission to be formed. The ten members of this commission, which included Dr. Kwegyir Aggrey, were sent to tour Tropical Africa to inquire into the state of education.

The scope of the inquiry was purposely made wide. The objectives were specified as follows:

1. to find out what and how much educational work was being done for the Africans in each of the territories visited.

2. to find out the educational needs of the people with reference to religious, social, hygienic and economic conditions, and ascertain the extent to which these needs were being met, and make suggestions as to how they might be best met. The commission was asked to publish its findings.

The commission visited the protectorate in 1924. It commended the missionaries for having made a good start despite very limited funds and staff, and noted that a lot remained to be done. It was thought that much of the weakness of the education system in Uganda was due to the absence of a government department of education and government inspectors of schools. It should be noted that the Protestant mission had after June 1904 set up a board of education whose functions were to handle all matters concerned with the education work of the Anglican Church in Uganda. The board was charged with the responsibility to advise on the building of schools and maintenance of existing ones, the supply of teachers, their remuneration and training, and the appointment of inspectors of Mission Schools.

The bishop was the chairman of the board. The Catholic mission too, had set up a machinery to administer their school system. The commission must have been made aware of the existence of these arrangements for the administration of mission education but perhaps found them, as missionaries themselves were willing to admit, inadequate and inefficient. Perhaps looking ahead, they were not likely to be capable of effecting a measure of unification for the country's education system and its administration in the future. Furthermore, missionary societies had tried to inspect their schools particularly the little ones but the arrangements were inadequate. The Phelps-Stokes Commission had this to say concerning mission inspection:

> By a mere enumeration of the Missionaries at work and the work they have to do, it has been proved without a shadow of doubt that Missionaries are not undertaking and cannot undertake the work of the inspection of schools in any way approaching adequacy.[1]

The reason for this state of affairs is not difficult to find. The pastors, the rural deans, just had no time for the proper inspection and administration of the schools under them although substandard they were in all ways. Furthermore, they had no qualifications for the work. Often their main interest, when they visited the school, was to see whether or not the preparation for Christian baptism or for confirmation was well conducted. It was, therefore, recommended that the protectorate government set up a department of education without further delay.

The Commission registered concern that the missionary societies had not related their educational activities to the community needs of the people. It was their considered view that the omission of teaching Agriculture, Health Science and Hygiene and the lack of provision for the instruction of women in the care of children was a very serious indication of the weakness of mission education which should not be let to continue. The government had to get involved in educational work and see to it that education activities were related to the needs of the children and the community. These particular remarks of the commission call for comment. First of all, the question is: To what extent should the remarks be taken seriously? It should not be forgotten that the main objective of the educational activities of the missionaries was "evangelization of the people" to be followed in time by their conversion and social uplift.

Before deciding to take the commission's remarks seriously, it is further important to remember that some places regarded as schools were not schools as such but centres of evangelisation and their programme was designed to make the pupils literate before baptism, and that was all. There was, therefore, no provision for Agricultural Education and Hygiene and Health Science classes.

Furthermore, it may be argued that to relate educational activities to the community needs of the people an Education Development plan is necessary. The missionaries did not have one nor did government. The remarks made by the commission were only useful in so far as they, at least, indicated that in future the community needs of the people should be taken into account by those engaged in educational activities. In their better and long established schools, missionaries taught Hygiene and Agriculture in the classroom often without outdoor practical demonstration this being the main shortcoming of the instruction thus given.

The commission severely criticised the free use of high-sounding names for schools whose actual standard was far below what the name suggested, and recommended that a new classification with Makerere at the top be carried out.

Missionary Contribution to Education up to 1925

The Phelps-Stokes Commission, as already indicated, criticised the missionaries. Other people have also criticized them. Three major criticisms have been made. Firstly, that the education which missionaries provided was too exclusively literary. This however seems to be an over-statement. It is not entirely true that missionaries provided exclusively literary education. Generally, manual work was obligatory in all mission schools. Even the teachers in some schools were expected to show practical ability in this area. For example, Mr. H.T.C. Weatherhead, the headmaster of King's College Budo, from September 1912, who himself having attended a course in handicraft before he came to this country, is reported when writing to a friend in 1912, to have said that Budo School wanted, if possible, a man who was handy and knew a little carpentry, so as to relieve him as headmaster, the handicraft classes. Obviously, there must have been handicraft classes, and the headmaster had been running them.

Earlier on in 1908, at a prize-giving day at Budo, the then headmaster had confidently reported on the Budo boys' favourable response to manual work when he said that pupils had maintained roads leading to the school and kept football fields and lawns trim and tidy. Incidentally, how many Budo pupils would do this now? Furthermore, the CMS Educational Scheme for Uganda in 1909, having among other things said that training which imparted book knowledge was not complete, stressed that eye, ear and hand must be trained and the educational value of labour must be taught. Missionary leaders stressed Manual training in their speeches and writings. For example, in 1922 Bishop Gresfford Jones, writing in appreciation of an experiment in technical education his colleague Archdeacon Mathers had conducted in Bukedi area, indicated the degree of emphasis when he wrote:

All Training Institutions must have manual training enthusiastically developed as an educational subject, and any teacher who is incompetent to give manual training or has not sufficient enthusiasm to do it, must be considered incompetent as a teacher. At all costs we must break down the idea that the village teacher or inspector is someone who is interested solely in the teaching of the three Rs. And if we are to get that impression, which exists everywhere, out of the heads of the people of Uganda, for some years to come it must be clearly seen that the teacher, and indeed all engaged in education, far from being solely interested in reading, writing, and arithmetic, are passionately concerned also with the development of hand and eye, and the training of the youth of Uganda to take part more effectively in agriculture, village industry, and animal husbandry, and in particular are interesting themselves in the bodily as well as the spiritual health of every boy and girl who attend any kind of school in the Protectorate.[2]

Also the White Fathers were in 1923, for instance, already successfully running St. Joseph's Technical School, a technical establishment next door to Kisubi College and yet another one at Bukalasa near the seminary. The work done in these institutions was purely technical. There was a wood work, shoe-making, tinsmiths' courses, courses for moulding roof and floor-tiles plus brick-making courses and training in printing and masonry. Although at first products of these institutions were meant to work for the missions, some of them eventually found themselves in the employment of the government or industrial firms.

It is for the reason that technical education was not adequately planned or organised that the criticism has arisen. But then it is unreasonable to expect the missionaries, painfully short of funds and qualified manpower ,to have done more than they did.

The second criticism has been that their school system lacked supervision. This was not untrue. As already indicated , they just did not have the staff to do it. Yet the third criticism has been that mission schools offered education which failed to fit the pupil for the village life. The point made here is that instead of making a pupil want to live in his village after he had been to school, mission schools tended to make him fit to live only as a clerk in town or wherever such work could be obtained. Mr. Ernest F. Spanton writing in 1928 three years after the period under review, offers a debatable explanation. He wrote:

Education for life is a phrase constantly used by Dr. Jesse Jones and many other writers who have followed him, and the principal objection to that literary education which was the characteristic of so many of the old fashioned Mission Schools is generally held to be that it failed to fit the African for the village life which would, in all probability, be his lot, because it disregarded to a large extent the conditions in which his life must be spent. For this reason our modern educationists demand the teaching of Hygiene, Agriculture and village handicrafts; for this reason vocational training looms large in our latest plans. But we must not allow ourselves or others ever to forget that these things, and others like them, considered singly or all together, do not of themselves form education for life; we should be doing the African a poor service were we to teach him how to earn his living but omit to teach him how to live; and only religion, touching his life at all points and including all its relationships, can do that.[3]

The criticism cannot be taken lightly nor does Spanton offer a satisfactory explanation. It should, however, be noted that without adequate funds missions could not possibly have given a technical and agricultural education to thousands of pupils in their schools. As many people may know, success has not been spectacular regarding pupils returning to land after school.

Remembering that missionaries were assisted only with very small grants from the government and therefore lacking adequate funds, they did a considerable amount of work for which they deserve credit. What they achieved can be briefly summarised as follows:-

1. Through their efforts, the country was covered with a network of schools. It is true that although some of these were no where near what a school should be, they at least afforded a foundation on which future developments could be based.
2. They stimulated popular interest in education among boys and girls and parents.
3. Generally speaking, although educational advance was slow, their educational system was broad-based.
4. Their school system made provision for pupils, able to do so, to move from the lowest to the highest step.
5. They established a close link between religion and education.
6. They provided the Administration with men who could do some clerical work.

The Phelps-Stokes Commission records that at least 177,000 pupils were attending mission schools in 1924. This was a remarkable achievement on the part of missions.

9

Government Begins to Participate Directly in Uganda's Education

Partly as a result of the report and recommendations of the Phelps-Stokes Commission, and partly as a result of the publication of the British Government White Paper on Education in Tropical Africa of 1925, which called upon government to pay close attention to education, the protectorate government realised that it was its duty to participate more directly in the difficult problems of Uganda's education which was by no standard adequate.

The First Director of Education Takes up his Duties 1925

The Governor, Sir Geoffrey Archer with the aid of a scheme for the participation of government in education which Mr. Eric J. Hussey, chief inspector of schools in Sudan had submitted to him in August 1924 after the study he had undertaken at the governor's request, set up a department of education in 1925. Hussey was seconded from Sudan for service in Uganda and took up his duties as the first director of education on the 15 February, 1925. Eric Hussey's arrival marked the beginning of the protectorate government's involvement in Ugandas' education. The government's move was in some quarters not welcome. Some Europeans were not happy about the increased expenditure on African education that would result from government's direct participation. Some Africans wondered what the government's motives were for interfering in a field that had been worked by missionaries alone for so many years. The missionaries, however, warmly welcomed the move, and their leaders spared no effort to impress on the doubters that government participation would in time provide resources that would give education a big leap forward.

In addition to the opening of the department of education, an Advisory Council on Native Education had been set up and by June 1925, this council included all provincial commissioners, representatives of the missions, as members.

Schools are Graded after the Arrival of the Director of Education

Under Hussey's direction schools throughout the country were carefully graded as follows:

1. Sub-grade schools. Schools in this group were not required to conform to a syllabus prescribed by government.
2. Elementary vernacular Schools. All schools in this category were required to use and follow strictly the syllabus as laid down by the government. Each school of this type was required to maintain a school garden for the purpose of instructing pupils in Elementary Agriculture to prepare them to live in the village.
3. Intermediate schools A and B. The most advanced schools of the missionaries were in the category labelled intermediate B, and they were by name, Kisubi, Budo and Namilyango. Central high schools were in the intermediate group A, and there were many of them.
4. Special grades: technical schools and normal schools were in this class. Normal Schools offered teacher training.
5. Makerere College: the highest institution, where professional courses could be taken and where teachers for intermediate schools would be trained.

Before the beginning of 1926 the majority of existing high and central schools were inspected, and during the year there was large-scale adjustment and change for missions. New names had to be adopted and classes had to be adjusted to the new prescribed syllabuses. All this seems to have gone on smoothly so that in 1927 the director of education was in a position to introduce the first Education Bill into the Legislative Council in December, 1927.

The Education Ordinance 1927

By the provision of this ordinance which the director of education described as an ordinance to provide for development and regulation of education, the existing education system was brought under government control. Although the government was not the owner and manager of schools it could, because of the ordinance, direct and determine what the owners could do in their schools and the type of teachers they might employ.

The ordinance empowered the director of education to register and classify all institutions at his discretion, to close schools not meeting the required standard, to impose fines on those who contravened the ordinance, to register teachers if they passed the examinations he prescribed and to strike off the register only teacher for repeated misconduct. He had, according to the ordinance, powers to visit any school at any time without notice and inspect it and anyone obstructing him would be liable to a fine of Shs. 1000. Provincial and district boards, which the ordinance set up and which were presided over by administrative officers, supervised schools.

Reaction to the Ordinance

While missions welcomed the ordinance to the extent that it would give them assistance in the huge task of building, financing, training of teachers and staffing of schools, and while they expressed willingness to use their influence to make it acceptable and workable, they however, wanted its enforcement delayed, criticism of it encouraged and responded to by way of accepting amendments. They were also particularly unhappy about its penal clauses and stressed that co-operation rather than fear of penalty would make the law happily workable and respected. The ordinance came into force on 1 September, 1928.

Impact of the Ordinance

The Director of Education, Hussey had at first hoped that mission, central and high schools might be taken over by his department but he soon found out that the colonial policy then did not provide for this. Indeed, after the ordinance, the curriculum, the objectives of schools, the ownership and their management were determined by the mission groups. The protectorate government avoided as much as possible owning schools. However, this is not surprising because the government had no explicit ideas and policy regarding African education. The voluntary agencies, on the other hand, having been in the field for quite a long time had formulated and strengthened their aims and policy as far as their schools were concerned that the ordinance had little impact.

Inspection, to which the ordinance attached so much weight and obstruction to which called for severe financial penalties, for a number of years remained merely a paper statement. The government found it impracticable financially to establish, and also had fears about establishing, an adequate inspectorate. The director's (of Education) 1933 report throws some light on the above suggestions. He reported thus:

> …. the lack of adequate supervision by the owners of certain mission schools is still causing anxiety. It is obvious that a missionary in these societies has so many duties that he is not able to devote time to school inspection work, while the ad hoc missionary educationist has usually a full time job in his own particular school. The financial difficulties of the last few years have been severely felt by most missions and there is a sad lack of men and money, in some cases resources which were essential to hold positions already won but not consolidated, are spent on new and more romantic enterprises. If efficiency is to be achieved and the accepted 'through the mission' policy is to be retained, it would appear the Government will be called upon to make a larger financial contribution by providing grants for mission supervisors, both European and African. The alternative is to have a largely increased government Inspectorate staff but this would be more expensive and a far less satisfactory method as it would tend to weaken co-operation between missions and government, and to undermine the religious bias which is such an essential factor.[4]

The above extract quoted out of the director's report shows to a considerable extent, how an ordinance whose provision made it appear as if it would have tremendous impact on the education system that, it actually had very little impact if any. Religious bias as stressed by the missions, remained an essential factor in education. The ordinance simply marked the beginning of the partnership between missions and government in the provision of education for Ugandans, the missions shouldering the burden of management, supervision, determining the goals and even staffing, while the government provided minimum grants-in-aid and overall but in may ways detached supervision. The schools belonged to the missions and operated on their aims, and this was accepted for such a long time that, when after independence the government of independent Uganda took these schools over, there was resistance on the part of some of the operators of the schools and even some parents did not refrain to demonstrate their feelings about the change in the status quo ante.

Type of Education Medium of Instruction in Schools

In the period 1925-1935, the two issues of the type of education to be offered and the medium of instruction which generated a lengthy debate and gave rise to some interesting experiments.

At the Legislative Council meeting of 28 May, 1926, a member of the council, Mr. H.H. Hunter, asked the director of education what steps were being taken by his department to train Ugandans in the skilled processes associated with the farming and planting industries. Hunter also wanted to know whether the education department had a scheme of apprenticeship for Ugandans desiring to learn skilled trade, drawn up by the education department. These questions indicated the feeling of a small group of people which included men like Hunter and a number of educators in the field, and the department of education, that as much as possible the education system for Ugandans should avoid too much academic training but should provide vocational education and prepare the majority of the pupils to live well in their villages.

Practical Aspect of Education stressed

The director of education, in his reply to Mr. Hunter, explained that the syllabus drawn up by his department for elementary vernacular schools for instance, provided two hours of practical training in Agriculture. Furthermore, there was a special agricultural course organised by an agricultural officer selected by the director of agriculture, as an integral part of the curriculum for the normal schools for training elementary school teachers. Agriculture would also figure prominently in the syllabus for higher schools. He also revealed that in the five-year programme of educational development there was provision for a technical school for training apprentices in various trades.

He further intimated that the General Manager of Kenya and Uganda Railways was willing to arrange for apprentices to be apprenticed to skilled workmen in his department. Eric Hussey the director, was a firm believer in vocational training and was openly anxious to cut down the number of mission schools which gave the usual academic training and to encourage the development of many post-primary schools into semi-vocational central schools.

Under Hussey's influence, in view of the education department the central schools, as they were called, were the most needed post-primary institutions for Uganda to absorb the bulk of the number of pupils after leaving the elementary vernacular schools. Consequently, a number of central schools were opened up and an attempt made to run vocational courses.

Central Schools to 1936

Fully developed central schools were post-elementary semi-vocational schools offering a 3-year or 4-year course to students for whom these schools were terminal. English was taught as a subject otherwise, the medium of instruction was either Kiswahili or, where possible, the vernacular of the area where the school was situated. There were on the time-table periods for Agriculture, Handiwork, Elementary Clerical and Commercial Studies (for example, typing). It was at one point even proposed to open and run shops at these schools to enable boys to get some practical idea of retail business. From 1935 teachers for these schools were mainly recruited from Kampala Normal School, a teacher training school set up by the protectorate government on Makerere Hill, Kampala.

Missionaries and articulate African opinion, while appreciative of the value of practical and manual education, considered it as inadequate preparation for leadership and the career needs of the pupils and opposed central schools. It is, obviously, hard to believe that practical and manual education would provide inadequate preparation for leadership. The central school experiment was generally abandoned soon after 1936. But, it must be pointed out that practical education was not cut out of the school programme as it has been erroneously suggested by some people on some occasions. It continued.

Up to 1939, at least, primary schools and secondary schools had school gardens and, wherever possible, a school had a teacher who had taken up a course at Bukalasa or Serere to help teach Agriculture at school. Schools like King's College Budo, had what was called 'the school farm' up to the 1950s. Besides including Agriculture in the curriculum for schools, there were farm schools established by the government at Bukalasa, Serere and Masindi which ran courses which were even attended by chiefs in the hope that they would help to spread better methods of farming in areas under their operation. No one could honestly say that work on school gardens was popular with the pupils. It was not, for the simple reason that digging with a hoe is no light job and is particularly arduous for young pupils. Furthermore, often interest that might have been generated and kept running was killed when teachers punished pupils by making them dig for certain periods in the school garden. It is well to point out, further, that parents, too, did not expect their children to be cultivators like themselves, they wanted them to take up clerical work or a job less exacting than digging, and one that carried prestige, after they left school.

It may also be added here that when the owners of schools were encouraged by the department of education to experiment with giving a more practical education at the middle school level to the majority of their pupils, in order to prepare them to live in villages, some of them did so with considerable zeal. Nyakasura High School under its headmaster, Commander E. Callwell, perhaps had the greatest success with the experiment. The school ran and maintained an electricity plant, laid on a water supply, ran courses in building and brick-making. Nor should the farm schools set up by the Protestant and Catholic Mission at Namutamba and Gulu respectively, be forgotten.

In 1938, the schools were classified again and the system set up then has, with very little modification, existed up to now. There were to be three types of institutions after 1938:
1. Primary school.   This provided a six year course, and English was the medium of instruction from form five.
2. Junior secondary school. A three-year course was provided.
3. Senior Secondary School. This offered a three-year course. After successfully completing the senior secondary school course and passing the entrance exams, students would proceed to Makerere College, an inter-territorial college for East Africa. Vocational education was to be provided by technical schools, and gradually courses in commercial studies were phased out of secondary schools.

What Should be the Medium of Instruction?
To a good number of people Kiswahili seemed to be the answer to this question. The governor in his communication to the secretary of state for the colonies for example, suggested that Kiswahili be adopted for the purpose of African elementary education, and for use in normal schools in the protectorate, and that Kiswahili be the language of instruction in the technical schools. Advocates of Kiswahili as a medium of instruction did not lack convincing arguments. Administrators particularly argued that there would certainly be advantages accruing from using what could easily become a lingua franca over East Africa.

The possession of a common language, they further argued, would give rise to better understanding between Uganda and Europeans, as local dialects were too many and very few Europeans knew any reasonable number of them. The director of education, Hussey, who argued consistently and persuasively for the use of Kiswahili, saw in it a medium of inter-tribal and inter-territorial communication. He felt that the Kiswahili language zone would be so wide that it would give impetus to the production of reading material. Books in Kiswahili would be accessible to all literate East Africans whereas, if they were in English, they would be read only by those who had been to schools and learnt English. All the arguments advanced in support of the use of Kiswahili, it seems, were sound although no one, Hussey included, would say to what extent Kiswahili facilitated learning. Would pupils learn faster and more effectively when taught in Kiswahili rather than in their vernaculars, for instance?

Opposition to the Use of Kiswahili

Among those who were opposed to the use of Kiswahili in schools was Mr. Rowling of the C.M.S. Namirembe, who expressed the fear that a widespread use of it would increase Muslim influence, and he labelled the move a political expedient. That Rowling should have taken this position is understandable: He had written quite a number of books in Luganda for which he and his supporters wrongly claimed flexibility and capability to meet the requirements of the school curriculum. Educationists like H. M. Grace, headmaster of Budo, without belittling the value of Kiswahili supported the use of English which they naturally regarded as the gateway to knowledge and as the likely lingua franca for the educated East Africans. But what about East Africans other than the 'elite'?

The debate went beyond the boundaries of Uganda and in May 1931, at the meeting of the Joint Parliamentary Committee on Closer Union of Kenya and Uganda, after the Ugandan witnesses had unanimously supported English rather than Kiswahili as the universal language for the country, it was indicated that English would be the lingua franca in future; and so it is. However, Kiswahili was taught as a second language according to a ruling of the department of education in Teso, Lango, Acholi, and West Nile and elsewhere as a subject, if so desired.

Nevertheless on the 7 August, 1973, the Government of Uganda declared Kiswahili to be the national language for Uganda, thus bringing the country in line with the rest of East Africa in terms of language.

10

Education in the Period 1939-1945

(a) The Education System

1. At the base of the educational system were sub-grade schools, which were unaided since the government found it impossible to ensure adequate supervision and the observance of minimum requirements. They were mainly staffed by unqualified teachers who taught no more than the 3 Rs and imparted religious instructions. The most promising pupils moved from these schools for further education.

2. Primary vernacular schools. These had better teachers and buildings than sub-grade schools, and provided instruction in the medium of the vernacular throughout the four years. The majority of pupils ended formal education at this level.

3. Primary schools. They offered a six-year course with English introduced in 5th year and used as medium of instruction in classes five and six. Each class was taught by a qualified teacher. Girls' primary Schools were practically all boarding and were headed by a European headmistress. The majority of boys' primary schools were day and had African headteachers.

4. Junior Secondary. This type of institution offered the first three years of secondary course.

5. Senior secondary schools. A 3-year course leading to the Cambridge School Certificate examination or what in those days was called Uganda Senior Leaving Certificate.

6. The government technical schools offered five-year post-primary practical courses in Carpentry, Building and Mechanics and 3-year courses in Tailoring. At least, in 1938 an experimental course in boat building was started at Kampala Technical School (in buildings now used by Makerere University Estates Department).

7. Teacher training was undertaken at levels. (i) There was a 2-year training course for teachers of sub-grade schools and the vernacular primary schools which was conducted at various places and the entry requirements to which was the completion of P.4. (ii) There was also a 3-year post-primary course to train teachers for primary schools and make available heads of primary vernacular schools. The course was conducted in English. (iii) Makerere College trained teachers for junior secondary schools.

8. Makerere offered inter-territorial post secondary courses in Medicine, Agriculture, Veterinary work and Engineering Science and Teacher Education.

(b) The War Time and its Effects on the Education System

Uganda Protectorate as part of the British Empire became involved in the Second World War as soon as it began. There was some dislocation of the education system which, however, did not give rise to serious results. About 19 European missionaries were called up for service and about 69 missionaries and 49 sisters who were nationals of countries with which Britain was at war were interned. Except for the Gulu Farm School, which closed down because of the internment of the European instructor, other places did not close down as arrangements were made for them to be administered by the educational secretary-general for Catholic mission schools. There was also loss of revenue from overseas and a reduction in the purchasing power of grants. It is safe to say that generally the school system did not suffer undue dislocation.

The war showed how schools can be used as vehicles of information for the community and as sources for direct contributions to services required by the Government. (1) The department of education in conjunction with the government information officer distributed news bulletins concerning the international situation to a number of schools for the eventual transmission to the homes of various communities. (2) Senior students of Kampala Technical School, supervised by their teachers, inspected and re-conditioned a considerable number of motor-vehicles requisitioned for war, built no less than 60 lorry-bodies and completed and painted 200 lorries. (3) Boy Scouts took part in guarding Kampala, thus relieving the police of guard duty. (4) Some schools under the direction of the agricultural department cultivated economic crops on what were styled 'war acres'.

Revenue from the sale of the crops was paid into the Uganda War Fund. By the end of 1941 the school contribution through this means was Shs. 20,000. (5) Recruiting authorities from East African Army Headquarters, requested and enlisted boys who had completed full primary or junior secondary courses as they were needed for semi-technical and technical section of the army. (6) Some African teachers of Makerere and primary standard were recruited, particularly in the period 1940-41, for service with the East African Army Education Corps, to teach African languages and method of dealing with African soldiers to European officers. (7) From January 1942, the mechanical section of Kampala Technical School was taken over by the army for turning out military artisans at the rate of 100 every three months. Motor vehicles fitters, blacksmiths, tin smiths and electricians were thus produced.

(c) The 1942 Education Ordinance

Changes which had taken place since the publication of the 1927 Education Ordinance made it necessary for a new education law to be made in 1942. The title of this important law was the 1942 Education Ordinance and one of the more important features of it which we would like to mention here was under section 56 which empowered the governor to prescribe the conditions governing the award of grants-in-aid. By virtue of the provision, in December 1943, the self-governing schools (grants-in-aid) rules were made to apply to all schools receiving grants-in-aid from public funds. The grant-in-aid was calculated on the basis of the school's estimated revenue and budget and it was intended to cover maintenance not covered by revenue from other sources.

The rules spelt out how such schools shall from that date be managed. There was to be a board of governors to control the educational policy of the schools in question subject to any general directions from the director of education and in consultation with the Advisory Council for African Education, and in religious matters subject to directions from the supreme denominational authority.

Each board of governors was to have a chairman nominated by denominational authority. There were to be 3 government nominees, and 3 nominees of the denominational authority. There would also be 5 members elected by the chairman and the nominated members. The chairman would remain in office as long as he was wanted by the denominational authority. A third of the members would retire at end of every school year but they would be required to present business to the board and attend all its meetings although he would have no vote. The board must meet at least once a year.

For the first time, the rules defined the duties of the headmaster as follows:-

1. He was to be personally responsible to his board of governors for the academic, social and domestic organisation and conduct of school.
2. It would be his duty to arrange curriculum and syllabus as required by the director of education.
3. It would further be his duty to arrange religious instruction and education under the guidance of denominational authorities.
4. He was to be responsible for the feeding, medical care and welfare of pupils and be in charge of all employees of the board.
5. He would be expected to make arrangements for the admission of pupils, to collect fees and to report failure to pay fees and all pupils discontinued on grounds thereof.
6. It was to be his duty to furnish the parent or guardian of every pupil entering school with the statement that pupils may be expelled from school on any grounds that are considered by the board to be in the interest of the school.
7. The headmaster was to furnish the board with an annual report, cause accounts to be kept and arrange for audit of school accounts.

Inspection of Schools

The rules made self-governing schools liable to inspection by panels of education officers. The chairman of such a panel, would after inspection meet the board of governors, to amplify the report and, after this, the report and comments on it would be submitted to the government.

11

Policy, Administration, Control and Development 1945-1962

Policy and Administration

It will be recalled that the protectorate government entered the educational field in 1925 signified by the appointment of the first director of education, Eric Hussey. Twelve years later in 1937 the director of education, in his annual report, stated the government education policy thus:

> The policy of the Government has been to develop and encourage missionary effort by (i) provision of direct grants to selected schools above the elementary standard, (ii) the establishment of District Boards to make recommendations for financing sub-grade and elementary schools and (iii) the inspection and supervision of Mission Schools. Normal schools have been established for the training of all grades of teachers. Facilities for higher education have been provided by the establishment of a Government College at Makerere and for technical education at 2 Government technical schools. Every effort is being made to impart an agricultural bias to education given in elementary and sub-grade schools. The Government is thus working through the missions doing all in its power to make schools effective. The marked progress and improvement made in recent years reflected the success of this policy of co-operation and are most encouraging to all concerned.[5]

The keynote in the development, administration and control of the educational system throughout the period under review was the "policy of co-operation". Every year, for a considerable period, each of the educational secretaries for CMS White Fathers, Mill Hill Fathers, Africa Inland Mission, and Verona Fathers, respectively, wrote a progressive report on schools under their charge which was included in the annual report of the department of education.

By the 1940s the Roman Catholic missions were co-ordinated for educational purpose under a single educational secretary-general whose office was at Nsambya in Kampala. Likewise, the Protestant missions' educational work was co-ordinated by one educational secretary-General whose office was situated on Namirembe Hill. Before the end of 1940s the Uganda Muslim Education Association started operating vigorously and it, too, had an educational secretary-general with his office on Kibuli Hill, and co-ordinating all Muslim schools in the country.

These educational secretaries-general were responsible for the administration of all schools under their charge, appointing area supervisors of schools, appointing headmasters and appointing teachers. They were also the negotiating agents with the protectorate government and local governments. Their influence over the administration and control of African schools under them (and the majority of schools was under them) was for a long time considerable. But the schools were denominational and for most of the time were used by members of the religious belief the Agency stood for.

If education was going to be one of the instruments to use, in order to create a national community, this state of affairs, it must be pointed out, was most unsatisfactory. Indeed, no education ordinance before 1964 was ever made giving powers to government to take over the direct administration of schools with educational secretaries-general excluded. For example, the 1942 Education Ordinance, regarded in official circles in those days as of considerable importance, did not charge the protectorate government with the administration of schools directly. By agreement with the mission concerned, and using powers conferred by the ordinance, government made six secondary schools and two teacher training centres, self-governing institutions with boards of governors representing both the religious authorities and government, with a provision for their annual budgets to be balanced by government grants. But all the same these institutions were still under education secretaries-general. Even at a later date, 17 years after the Ordinance, and even after a ministerial system of government had been established, and even after more secondary schools (besides the original six) had been made self-governing, in the education department annual report for the year ended 31st December 1959, the director of education reported as follows:

> All Senior Secondary Schools, the Kampala Technical Institute, training colleges and technical schools, all with their Boards of Governors are direct grant schools, aided from Central funds. The majority of those were originally founded by voluntary agencies; the channel of administration is then from Departmental Headquarters to the Board of Governors through the office of the Educational Secretary-General of the appropriate Voluntary Agency.[6]

Furthermore, the local educational authorities provision for whose establishment was made by the 1942 Education Ordinance, and regarded as far reaching, were not school owning bodies. While it is true they were charged with the planning and development of primary education, and selected unaided schools in their areas for addition to the list of aided schools, the administration of schools still rested with the voluntary agencies up to 1964.

No doubt the policy of co-operation between protectorate Government and voluntary agencies really lasted long.

Protectorate Government Reluctant to Take over Schools but Prepared to Direct and Develop Education

Although reluctant to take over direct administration of schools, the protectorate government directed and made effort to develop the educational system for Uganda. Particularly in the 1950s because of the wish of Governor Sir Andrew Benjamin Cohen to spread out development opportunities to different parts of Uganda, the protectorate government started building its own secondary schools to stand side by side with mission secondary schools. Schools like Ntare School, Teso College Aloet, Sir Samuel Baker, and Kigezi College appeared on the scene as a result. This was a welcome move because for a long time some people wanted to see schools free from mission control built. These new schools also got Board of Governors appointed to them.

De Bunsen Reports on Education in Uganda 1953

Again Sir Andrew governor (1952-1956) having stressed that economic expansion would be impossible unless accompanied by social and political advancement, appointed a committee under the chairmanship of Mr. B. de Bunsen, then Principal of Makerere College to investigate and report on the state of education and submit proposals for the future organisation and development of education in Uganda. The de Bunsen Committee made three major recommendations:-

1. There should be a vigorous re-organisation of the teacher training system, involving raising the entrance qualifications and reducing the number of teachers' colleges from 41 to 23 for efficiency.
2. The senior secondary course to be reduced to four after an 8-year primary course.
3. Local education authorities, i.e. district councils to be responsible for primary education.

The committee also studied teachers' conditions of service and recommended new pay scales. This had been long overdue and all over the country teachers were unhappy about what they were paid for the heavy duties they faithfully carried out.

The government accepted and gradually implemented the committee's recommendations.

Main Developments After the de Bunsen Committee's Report

1. Expansion of the education department.
   The year 1952 when the de Bunsen Committee was appointed the education department was staffed as follows:-

(a) Headquarters (i)   The director of education,'

            (ii)   The deputy director of education,

           (iii)   Plus a very limited number of education officers.

(b) In the field were:

4 provincial education officers for Buganda, Northern, Eastern and Western Provinces. Eastern Province also had one woman education officer for organising Domestic Science. There were also 6 education officers, and 15 assistant education officers.

Provincial education officers carried out the following duties:-

Inspection, grant-in-aid list compilation, preparing estimates for districts, and attending meetings of local education authorities. The de Bunsen Committee recommended that the education department should be expanded. In 1953 there were signs of the implementation of this recommendation.

1. At the headquarters the staff was as follows:-

The director of education, deputy director of education, a deputy director (technical), an assistant director, (women and girls), an inspector of schools, and a superintendent of teacher training. This, hitherto, unusual increase in staff, enabled the director of education to establish 4 sections at headquarters namely: Technical education section, secondary education section, teacher training (education) section and Education of girls and women section. In the field as previously, there were 4 provincial education officers, but the number of education officers was raised to 24 as against 15 in 1952.

2. The cut-down in number of teacher training colleges as recommended by de Bunsen Committee was implemented, making it possible to equip and staff the remaining colleges more adequately.

3. An 8-year primary school and a 4-year secondary course were adopted. As a result junior secondary classes 1-3 were removed and established some where in the neighbourhood - to make room for double streaming of all senior secondary courses, with the doubling of secondary school output as the objective.

4. Following the de Bunsen Committee recommendation, African local government or district councils became the local education authority replacing local education authority set up in accordance with provisions of the 1942 Education Ordinance, i.e. ad hoc committees. The new local education authority would appoint an education committee for day-to-day business, with the education officer as its secretary. The de Bunsen's recommendation that voluntary agencies be represented was accepted and implemented by allowing the provincial commissioner to nominate 50 per cent of the committee as

representatives of voluntary agencies and the rest nominated by the district council from other sources.

But there was a considerable amount of "dragging of feet" over the question of local education authorities assuming full responsibility over primary education. The education department did not seem to want to see immediate implementation of this, for, in his annual report for 1953 the director of education wrote:

> The Voluntary Agencies, particularly on the Protestant side, maintain, reasonably enough, that if the Local Education Authorities are to assume responsibility for primary education it is right that they should assume also responsibility for the managerial, inspection, and clerical functions of supervisors, and they are prepared to hand over these duties to Local Education Authorities as soon as possible. The successful assumption of such duties, however, will be an educative process involving a considerable period of time, and as an interim measure it is proposed that all African supervisors, assistant supervisors and clerical staff appointed in the immediate future should be engaged as Voluntary Agency employees posted for duty to various Voluntary Agencies' supervisors with whom they will work but with an overall responsibility to the Local Authority. When the time arrives for handing over full responsibility to the Local Education Authority together with the secondment of staff, these African supervisors and clerical assistants may be seconded to the service of the Authority and new appointments will eventually be made to the Authority's permanent service, not on secondment. [7]

There is no need at all to comment on this statement at length, for it was not until 1964 after the colonial period that Voluntary Agency supervisors of schools were kicked out of the system.

Supervision and Inspection of Schools

The de Bunsen Committee wanted the policy of co-operation to continue, and over the question of supervision and inspection of schools, while recommending that the latter be a duty of the department of education the former, it was felt, should remain a function of voluntary agencies. The functions of supervisors need spelling out and we do so here. While they operated, their sphere of activity included managerial and inspection (not professional) functions plus visiting teachers, advising or reprimanding them upon their personal problems in the light of mission principles. Some teachers were never happy with visits from the supervisors.

(iv) Local Authorities and Education 1952-64

As already mentioned in this account, the de Bunsen Committee proposed that responsibility for primary education be devolved upon African local authorities (i.e. district councils or in case of Buganda – Kabaka's Government). While the government found this proposal acceptable, it required two conditions fulfilled before responsibility of primary education could be handed over to local authorities.

1. That each education committee draws up a 5-year development plan for the district and on the lines of policy laid down for all Uganda and within the limits of finances likely to be available for education.
2. That there must be available for the secondment to the district concerned, appropriate administrative staff viz, the education officer.

Surprisingly, the somewhat hard conditions laid down by central government did not deter local authorities from work. In a good number of cases, education committees set up development sub-committees to study and tender advice on all aspects of their educational plans. These sub-committees seem to have taken their charge seriously and their systematic approach to the problems of executing an educational development plan merited appreciation at the departmental headquarters. Generally, in all districts, development plans tackled the question of upgrading P4 schools to P6 schools first, and then the upgrading of P2 schools to P4 schools and then considered starting new schools. Local authorities, as time went on, found the idea of working to a 5-year development plan good, since even if changes in departmental or mission personnel took place the plan was there to be followed.

Furthermore, education committees in all districts paid particular constructive attention to allocation to educational purposes of special funds made available by the district or kingdom or African local government. Special funds, it will be recalled, were raised in the form of education tax which was, for instance, shs 5 in Buganda. Education committees allocated funds thus raised to building of staff houses, absolutely necessary, and school buildings. In some districts committees went further. They allocated funds to bursaries and scholarships to students to study at secondary school and even in a limited number of cases to study abroad.

Some committees used funds to award prizes in schools for the encouragement of certain activities. Lango District Education Committee, for example, offered prizes for a school gardens' competition which was favourably reported on by the provincial education officer, Northern Province, regarding its effect on school garden standards in the district. The 1959 Education Ordinance gave local authorities further **encouragement.**

(v) The Administrative Set-up in 1959

The year 1959, when the already mentioned Education Ordinance was made, and just three years before Uganda gained her independence, the administration set-up was more or less what it had been in previous years except for one additional and important development at headquarters.

At headquarters (1) the director of education was now responsible to the minister of education and labour (ministerial government had started in September 1955) and was charged with the control and administration of the educational system.

(2) He was assisted by:
   (i)   a deputy director (professional matters)
   (ii) a deputy director (technical)
   (iii) 3 assistant directors and a number of officers.

(3) A separate inspectorate had been started but at the same time, as the majority of schools were still managed by voluntary Agencies viz Protestant, Catholic Missions and the Uganda Muslim Education Association, and as had been the case for many years, each of these agencies had an elaborate organisation for the administration and supervision of its schools. There were provincial education officers in Northern, Western and Eastern Provinces each divided into districts with an education officer in charge of a district – assisted by an assistant education officer.

For Buganda the position had changed. Under the Buganda Agreement of 1955, a Ministry of Education had been set up and a minister appointed his permanent Secretary a senior education officer on secondment from central government, and a standing committee of the *Lukiiko* Parliament advised him. Instead of district education officers there were divisional education officers. This roughly was the state of affairs up to 1961.

12

The Development of Agricultural and Technical Education

(a) Agricultural Education

All along, those operating Uganda's education system have made provision for giving agricultural education to the pupils. As mentioned in an earlier chapter, some courses in agriculture were taught in missionary schools. The charge that there was deliberate official indifference to the subject in schools is difficult to substantiate as syllabuses for primary schools and junior secondary schools, which included agriculture and keeping school gardens, were maintained at many of the schools. If the lessons did not cause pupils to love agriculture so as to make it their life career, that is another matter.

It would be dishonest, for example, to disregard the efforts of Government in the period 1939-1960 to give agricultural knowledge to school pupils. It will be recalled that by 1940 there was a government senior agricultural officer charged with the responsibility of seeing to the development of agricultural education in schools. Furthermore, government farm schools at Bukalasa, Gulu, Serere, Namutamba and Masindi trained agricultural demonstrators who were posted to villages to help all engaged in agriculture including school leavers who might have taken up work on the land.

Farm schools also provided courses of instruction in agricultural methods for pupils other than demonstrators. There were pupils also graduating from these farm schools who were not meant to be demonstrators. Such pupils, on leaving farm schools, were followed up by their instructors to see their progress and give them further help. The department of agriculture was charged with the duty of giving demonstration lessons in agriculture to teachers who would go on to teach the pupils in the primary schools and this was carried on extensively during refresher courses arranged on the farm schools.

Generally, people in charge of schools were warmly enthusiastic about agricultural training of their pupils. For instance in 1948, headteachers had a conference which advised that to every primary school should be attached a post-primary class, which should give training in agriculture and handicrafts to pupils who were not going on to the academic secondary schools and that, in secondary schools there should be manual instruction for all pupils. As a result of this, several secondary schools developed school farms, extended gardens and increased the amount of agricultural training offered. What more could have been done?

Some of the people who attended school between 1939 and 1960 were not employed elsewhere but went back to the land, and it seems the agricultural education they received at school had some impact on their approach to agriculture. There is evidence to show that agriculture during this period did change for the better. Land conservation was practised, crop rotation was adopted, new crops were introduced and grown extensively and pruning of plants and pest control were carried out. If some school leavers hated agriculture and therefore, consequently ran away from it, the cause of this was not because of absence of agricultural education. It was because of some other reasons which we mention here briefly. First, in many schools it was necessary to grow food and in all schools it was necessary to keep the compound tidy. Both these tasks were inescapable parts of schools routine especially in primary schools and they involved a great deal of hard and uninteresting work for both teachers and pupils. Quite often a period marked agriculture on the time-table could be spent by pupils working on the compound or weeding the school's food crop garden or collecting grass to thatch the teacher's house.

Much of this work included no interesting agricultural methods and it was all sheer manual and exhausting work. Worse still, as already briefly mentioned, punishing children tended to be thought more effective if a pupil was told to dig in the school garden. This was a form of punishment very much practised by teachers. In both ways pupils never used the agricultural techniques learnt in lessons. Their concern was to hurry through the drudgery, caring nothing about the techniques taught. This kind of punishment created hatred for agriculture among the young children since it was those who either failed at their lessons or who did something wrong who were supposed to do this exercise.

The argument could be pushed a step further that some pupils looked at cultivating the land as an unworthy exercise meant for wrong doers and people who had not gone to school or who had done so but had failed to distinguish themselves at their lessons.

Again it may be added that while nearly 90 per cent of the population was (and is to-day) engaged in agriculture, education was regarded as a process by which its recipients would escape from this basic activity into white collar positions. Parents hoped that their children should get qualifications and get white collar jobs. Children aspired to the same thing and the whole community felt the same way. If a boy especially, went to school and after completing his primary or junior secondary course returned to take up a hoe, he was branded a failure by the neighbours. So, the determination of those children who went to school was to 'graduate' and get paid employment in town or in government departments scattered all over the country.

The impetus to this determination lay in the fact that all people who were rising rapidly were those in white-collar jobs. The cultivator was rising very slowly despite the fact that he worked so hard. Here the prices of the crops were involved. Though the post-war period saw rising prices for farmer's produce, they never rose high enough except for about three years between 1951 and 1955. If this price had kept stable we believe the result would have been to attract a lot of people to take to cultivating more extensively and intensively and to attract the young to stay on the land despite their having paper qualifications from school. The time allocation to aspects of education in the education system gave the feeling that academic education was more valuable than practical education because of the fact that at school more time was allotted to academic work and when exams came agriculture was hardly examined. All this encouraged the feeling that it was not valuable. Even teachers were not too keen to teach Agriculture as a subject because it demanded a lot of ingenuity and physical exertion and there was little literature in simple language to read for guidance.

It was also unfortunate that some students who had training at schools of agriculture such as Bukalasa, Arapai and Makerere, often failed to start progressive farms themselves so that people might be convinced that one could make a decent living out of agriculture even if one had received formal training in our schools. The products of agricultural schools became administrators in government agricultural departments so that their earnings never depended on the changes of the weather or of the prices of crops. A lesson could be better learnt if a section of such people went into direct farming and convinced the people of the viability of cultivating the land. Nor did the farm school project produce long-term serious farmers.

During the 1950s the educational department started a system of farm schools. These were schools to which pupils completing primary education with no other place to go to, went to round off their education for two years. They learnt crop and animal husbandry so as to be effective and efficient farmers. The course included carpentry and smith work to produce competent farm men.

It also included farm arithmetic and simplified instructions in costing and accounting. However, there were two difficult problems. At the end of the course, making efficient arrangements for settling the pupils on their own farms in some districts was not easy, and once the land was obtained, keeping these boys on the holdings for long, was equally problematic. There was firstly, lack of capital for equipment and seeds. Also ex-students needed supporting rather more heavily during the first years of their existence as independent farmers until their farm began to yield produce which would be sold and the proceeds used for further development or to pay off capital loans. Some of the farm schools made simple tools and seeds available to trainees on completion of their training, others set aside a part of the proceeds from sales of produce for him to use on completion of the course. All farm schools provided an initial advisory service and some cases this lasted for a year whereby a member of staff visited the newly established farmer to discuss his problems. Schools possessing mechanical equipment also helped their ex-students to clear and break in new land.

But by 1960 the future of these farm schools was in the balance for fewer and fewer pupils were joining them and their impact on the public was not being felt for, after 'graduation' the students soon deserted their plots of land. After 1960 the farm schools were abandoned and only farm institutes such as Bukalasa and Arapai were left to produce administrators at a lower level and Makerere Faculty of Agriculture at a higher level. Instead of farm schools, district farm institutes were adopted which would give short courses to farmers in each district and also follow them up. Such were the efforts made in our education system to teach agriculture between 1939 and 1960. Any attempt of introducing agriculture in our schools in future needs to have this background clearly set before us.

(b) Technical Education

We have already in this account mentioned efforts to get technical education in Uganda going. The efforts we have mentioned have often not been appreciated and there has always been a feeling among many people that technical education was not adequately cared about by the colonialists. We suspect that what has given rise to this feeling is the direction whose pursuits of a purely academic nature have taken over both agricultural and technical education in our schools. Jobs, especially in the protectorate administration and in the local administration, and in the teaching profession, were more readily available for Ugandans with academic qualifications rather than those who had technical education. Indeed, in the period under review, a boy went unwillingly to the Kampala Technical School after he had failed to get into a school offering a purely academic curriculum. Many parents looked at the technical school as an institution for those who had no mental capacity for a regular secondary school course.

Despite all this, the education department and missionaries kept operating the technical schools they had set up. During the 1939-45 War the technical schools of the department of education were taken up to train recruits in some skills which they were going to use on the war front, while mission technical schools continued to educate students who were not going to the war. After the War, the government technical schools were used to give further skills of a practical nature to many demobilised ex-servicemen who cared to enrol for courses in them so that skills obtained in the war would be put to peace time use in the community. By 1950 this exercise was completed and the ex-servicemen in these technical schools passed out into public life as useful members of the society. The government technical schools which were located in all towns of Uganda reverted, after this exercise, to the department of education to be used as technical schools in peace time.

From 1950 to 1960 efforts to increase and improve facilities for technical education were intensified in order to diversify the education given in Uganda schools. The efforts were justified by the increased demand of people with technical skills in industry in the country. A technical advisory committee was set up in 1950 by government to advise it on the needs of industry in order to design the educational courses accordingly. It was found that there was a high demand for artisans. Plans were, therefore, made to start technical work from the primary section up to secondary school level to produce people with the technical skills demanded. The government appointed a British superintendent of technical education in 1950 and another British education officer in charge of manual training and £1million was set aside to help this development.

At primary level, boys were taught skills in the manufacture of handicrafts, such as chairs, baskets, mats and other artistic items needed in a home so that if they stopped schooling after primary education, they would be capable of bettering their homes or even earn a living by producing such articles in large quantities. Girls were taught what was called home crafts that is, making mats, carpets, brooms, sewing and some pottery. Special buildings like carpentry shops for handiwork were set up in primary schools and carpentry was taught by a carpenter who often knew no methods of teaching.

By and large, the success of all these technical and agricultural subjects in primary schools depended on the keenness of the headmaster and his staff. Where both were not so keen there were no results and this happened to be the case in most primary schools and the academic side of education gained favour and much support. Probably this was a fault traceable back to teacher training schools. Technical training was given a third place in importance in teacher-training institutions and so teachers graduated with half-baked ideas about teaching practical subjects in a society that had been made to feel that it was the academic subjects that mattered.

When time came to teach these subjects, teachers told pupils to just go and collect materials from the nearby forest or jungle. When the materials were brought the pupils were instructed to do what each one felt he had the ability to do with it. So some made ropes, others brooms, others stools and mats and rafia carpets drawing from the knowledge they had from their parents back at home. In many cases they were not taught or even shown how profitable such activities would be in later life. Pupils treated the exercise as a diversion from the "more useful" occupation of dealing with books. The majority of teachers during the period of handiwork would be marking exercise books or reading something or talking familiarly with their pupils who were working drawing from the home knowledge.

The result was that in may cases nothing new was taught and pupils hardly saw the usefulness of the exercise. That the exercise never had impact on the boys and girls was often indicated by the fact that after they had left school they often had to buy such articles as mats and brooms from other people rather than make them themselves. Examples of men who had done some woodwork at school but who in their own homes could not repair even a simple chair were common. At the next stage were established a number of rural trade schools called "round off" institutions like the farm schools. These rural trade schools took in students from Primary Six and gave them suitable technical training to add to their worth as country dwellers. These were supposed to go back to the land and were not supposed to look for jobs in towns. Then they would use this skill as country artisans in their homes. Girls attended home craft centres where they were prepared to be good wives and mothers. The unfortunate thing was that after the completion of the course, the boys tended to go to towns and look for employment instead of settling in the countryside and practise their crafts. In town they competed with boys who had formal technical training in technical schools. As a result the exercise of these "rounding off" schools was fruitless.

At the next stage junior secondary technical schools were started. Some were set up and managed by the protectorate government, some by the local governments and others by the missions. These were largely concerned with the training of artisans for industry. At first the standard of entry to these schools was Primary Six, later on it was raised to junior secondary Three. Training at this type of school was followed by training in industry and by a system of apprenticeship as recommended by the Advisory Council on Technical Education and by Dr. Harlow, assistant technical adviser to the colonial office in 1951. Yet many industries were not interested in engaging apprentices.

There were some academic junior secondary schools which included technical subjects in their curriculum, also in the hope that on completion the students would join higher technical schools after their junior secondary education. At the next stage there was a four-year course given at the Kampala Technical Institute which was established in 1955 when the Old Public Works Engineering School was incorporated. Courses at the Kampala Technical Institute were to lead to the School Certificate in practical subjects or to an ordinary diploma in commerce, engineering or building. After successful completion of this course students were eligible for entry into the Royal Technical College Nairobi which had been opened in 1956, to read for a degree in appropriate subjects. Kampala Technical Institute conducted from 1954 courses for technical teachers to remedy the great shortage of African technical instructors.

Research has shown that there were opportunities offered to Ugandans in technical training by the education system. It would be dishonest to dispute this. But the sad thing is that the opportunities were not exploited fully. We are inclined to think that some of the reasons for this state of affairs were as follows:-

1. The courses offered were inadequate for the reason that in many places the calibre of the instructors was shockingly mediocre. Many times the students who went to the courses in technical schools were discouraged by the

instructors who seemed to be unable to teach them effectively. As a result, very few students passed the prescribed public exams.

2. Boys who successfully completed the courses were much discouraged when they found that in industries, government and commercial departments, they were made assistants of Asians and Europeans who held lower qualifications or sometimes no qualifications at all, since in colonial days it was always the White man first, the Asians second and the African last. Consequently, the courses though desirable became unattractive.

3. The low status accorded to graduates of technical institutions by the society discouraged many to take up technical training.

The inadequacy of technical courses especially at the Kampala Technical Institute made the students there go on strike in 1957 complaining that the institute's teachers and their courses were not up to the standard and that the courses were designed to produce a cadre of African assistants subordinate to the Asians and the Europeans. The strike, however, was suppressed by the colonial government and the ring leaders were dismissed and the government affirmed that the courses were very adequate and very good.

Besides the technical instruction carried on in schools there were government departments which gave such training to those students who went to them after the completion of their academic courses in the secondary schools. These were being groomed to be future workers of the respective departments. The lands and survey department, the veterinary department, the lands and mines department, the posts and telegram and the public works department, all had training schemes of a technical nature and very many young men became efficient technicians as a result of the courses which they followed in these departments subsequent to their being employed by those same departments.

13

Segregation in Education and the Rise of Private Schools

(a) Segregation

Like elsewhere in East Africa, there was racial segregation in education. There were separate schools for Africans, Indians, Goans and Europeans and separate organisational and administrative arrangements. The Europeans had only one primary school in Kampala and sent their children to Kenya for secondary education. It was the Asians who had several primary and secondary schools. In Uganda there was no strict racial segregation as in Kenya, and to a little extent in Tanganyika. In fact, in Uganda some children of all races were admitted to any of the three categories of schools as and when circumstances and agreement between the parents and the school owners had made this desirable and possible. European children, for example, from time to time were educated at Budo, Asian pupils studied at African schools notably at Kisubi, Namagunga and Namilyango and Goan schools were always opened to children of all races. Asian children were admitted to various African schools and so were African children to Asian schools in towns throughout the country. It was, however, very difficult for African children to get places in European schools because of the language problems.

In 1957 African members of the Legislative Council called for integration of the schools, feeling justifiably that the situation was no longer acceptable. As a result of this demand the advisory councils on African, Asian and on European education discussed the issue of integration. But these councils, notably the Asian and the European ones, gave a lukewarm welcome to the proposals of integration. They contended that integration was likely to impair the European and Asian schools. They could, therefore, allow not more than five per cent African children in their schools. Indeed, these two racial groups feared an influx of African children into their schools to the extent that probably their children would not get places and they also wanted to keep the traditions of their schools, purely Asian or purely European.

After the discussion of the councils, the government made a policy statement that all primary and secondary schools should be non-racial and pupils should be admitted into schools on merit rather than on the basis of race. But the policy was radical on paper only. It was watered down in application by the director of education, a European himself and who naturally had to side with the European and Asian groups. He, for instance, said:

> In introducing this policy due regard must be had to the interest of the groups for which the peculiar schools were originally provided and for this reason it would be necessary for the process of integration to be gradual. The needs of such groups must continue to be met as at present; it is essential, too that where schools have developed particular traditions and characteristics, these should not be prejudiced. Equally, there must be no lowering of standards in any school.[8]

Integration remained on paper until independence.

(b) The Rise of Private Schools

By definition independent private schools are those educational institutions that are not financially aided in full or in part by the State. In 1925 the first independent private school started by Rev. Father Spartas Mukasa near Bombo appeared on the scene. From 1925 up to 1960 there were many mission schools that were not getting grants from the government, yet these mission schools were not called private schools. The term then was given to those schools started by lay men and by other christian churches in Uganda which were neither Roman Catholic nor CMS or the Native Anglican Church (NAC) of Uganda. By and large, this term was on many occasions used by the Roman Catholic and the NAC hierarchies to show their contempt for these schools.

Their starters and operators were looked at as rebels against the quasi-official established missionaries who provided education in Uganda. Secondly, the term was used to indicate that such schools were giving an inferior kind of education offered also in inferior surroundings. All this must have been done in a bid to discourage individual laymen in Uganda from setting up their own schools and also to discourage parents from sending their children to such schools because these schools were non-denominational and not committed to teaching religion.

That the opposition of the Roman Catholic and of the CMS missionaries was defeated and the independent private schools movement became an important force in offering education, shows that in Uganda there were men determined to see that these schools become established side by side with the missionary and the government schools. Also, it shows that there were parents in Uganda society who were ready to send their children to private schools to get the cherished school education despite the opposition of the two bodies named above at the beginning and despite the stigma which they tried to attach to them.

During the period under review, the independent private schools movement gained strength because there was a great demand for schools both primary and secondary and the missions and the government could not satisfy this demand. These schools were outside the grants-in-aid system and they grew purely the financial support of their owners who were predominantly Africans and who sacrificed a lot of personal comfort to run them. This was despite the fact that they used the school fees which normally tended to be higher than those in the missionary grant-aided schools.

By 1950 the number of these independent private schools had grown so much that the government was forced to recognize their presence and, therefore, decided to put some control on them in order to safeguard the interests of the parents. In 1951, the government appointed an officer to help them organize themselves and also to help them follow the established educational standards. From the mid 1950s these schools which had begun as primary schools, started providing secondary school education, because many parents had realised that to get a job a child needed secondary education. Yet the government and mission secondary schools were too few to satisfy the demand. At the same time, students were coming from the rest of East African states and from Zambia, Malawi, South West Africa and from southern Sudan to join these private secondary schools because in those parts opportunities for secondary education were still much limited.

Running a private school became a business lucrative. Soon after 1960, Asians joined in the race to set up private schools for two reasons. One reason was that due to the high demand for secondary education, which demand could hardly be satisfied by government, establishing private schools especially in towns was a gainful financial undertaking. The second reason was that in 1963 the government abolished racial and denominational schools. Many Asians children could not get enough places in secondary schools, whereas in the past due to so many places that were in their separate schools any Asian child who completed the primary school and wanted to go on for secondary education got a place.

Now, the Asians council saw that their children, who could not score the marks demanded by government to allow them to get into a government secondary school, would have no secondary education. So they established private schools to meet this need. These schools at the same time accepted African children in order not to look racial. Today there are more private schools especially at secondary level, than government-aided ones. This indeed can be understood under the present circumstances where for example in 1970, 80,000 pupils sat for the Primary Leaving Examination and government secondary schools could take only about 15,000.

14

Disparities in the Education System

(a) Female Education Lags Behind

Throughout the period 1900-60 there was great disparity between the number of boys and girls attending school and it was widespread although its magnitude differed from area to area. The causes of this disparity were several. Priority was usually given to boys by parents when funds were insufficient for both boys and girls. The domestic duties which girls had to carry out at home after school made their school attendance irregular and reduced their tenacity for learning. Girls generally used to go to school at a comparatively more advanced age than boys. They also tended to marry early. So, the length of the school career for most girls was often very short. Thus parents who looked at education as a form of investment thought better to invest in boys than in girls. Also, parents complained of the lack of adequate openings for girls after they had left schools. They contended that all girls did not wish to become teachers or nurses and they could not easily become clerks in offices as men did.

Indeed, this kind of thinking showed that many parents had as yet no appreciation of the fact that an educated girl would make a better citizen, wife and mother even if she got no paid employment. After all only a few boys got employment after schooling. Finally, the shortage of women teachers in mixed schools caused lack of attention to girls because men teachers apparently gave more attention to boys, who were more regular in attendance and showed greater enthusiasm for lessons. Often male teachers still thought that the work of women was in the home and therefore school education was less necessary for them. The lack of a sufficient number of women teachers in mixed schools was associated mostly with the Native Anglican schools and with the Muslim schools which practised co-education more extensively as a rule, than the Roman Catholic schools. In Roman Catholic schools co-education was not readily acceptable especially after the catechumen classes. Catholics would argue that girls had a different role to play in society which was quite dissimilar to that of boys. Girls should, therefore, be taught separately. Secondly, it was erroneously thought that morals in schools would be better if boys and girls studied separately. Catholic girls' schools fared well as far as women teachers were concerned, for besides employing lay women teachers, they also engaged large numbers of religious women who had vowed to remain unmarried all their lives. This contributed to stability in Catholic girls schools because lay women teachers, either Protestants or Catholic generally taught for a shorter period and then got married. After getting married many tended to stop teaching.

The government tried to give favourable terms to girls in order to attract them to schools. It gave them extra financial assistance by providing boarding facilities so they could be away from home, and so be free from the pressure of home chores. However, the existence of boarding facilities for girls, many times, did not always mean that the places were taken up. Secondly, again to help girls' education, the education department increased the number of post-primary homecraft courses for girls so that there might be chances for those who attended them to get employment. Wherever possible, at least two women teachers were posted to mixed schools. Due to these arrangements, and due to a gradual change in parents' attitude, by 1960 girls education had been stepped up so much that the number of girls in primary schools was 161,721 while that of boys was 354,027. Furthermore, by this year there were many chances for girls to be employed in offices.

In some districts, for every two boys there was a girl in primary school. But at secondary school level the number of girls continued to grow at a very slow pace. For example, by 1960 there were only 485 girls in secondary school but 3360 boys in the top three classes of the secondary schools.

(b) Education of Muslim Children Lags Behind

The disparity in numbers of boys and girls attending schools aside there was again disparity religion-wise and the most affected affiliation was the Muslim children. The Catholic and the Protestant children alike, attended school in large numbers. This was due to the fact that their missionary groups had established schools in competition with each other from the very beginning of the introduction of Christianity in Uganda. For example, no sooner had the Catholic mission established a school in an area than the Protestant mission followed suit and vice versa.

Where both groups saw no need to compete meant that, that area would have few schools and either one of them would put up a school there or the area would be neglected completely by both so that pupils would have to walk long distances to an area where those two denominations were competing keenly.

But the Muslims from the beginning of the Uganda Protectorate in 1894 had more or less stuck to the Koran system of schools. Some men who wanted their children to get the Western kind of education would send them either to catholic or Protestant schools. This was not always easy as operators of mission schools regarded them as a reserve for members of their faith. Yet schools for Muslim children on the lines of the types of schools run by Christian missionaries grew very slowly after they were started by far-sighted Muslim men who had got education in either Catholic or Protestant schools and who had realised in the

1920s and 1930s that under the colonial set up their children could not hope to vie on equal terms with Christian children for opportunities unless they followed an education system similar to that of the Christians. These Muslims began setting up their own schools and to give Muslim children secular education after their Koran education. This exercise was not easy for the pioneers because other Muslims who did not like to see such schools set up, feared that they would give rise to bad influence. On several occasions Muslim school buildings and even the pioneers' houses were burnt down, but the pioneers persisted and succeeded in the end.

The protectorate government, seeing the educational disparity that was bound to come about in the long run between Muslims one side, and Christians came to the aid of the pioneers. It set up a teacher training school for the Muslims in the mid 30s at Kasawo, 57 kilometres from Kampala in the then East Mengo District of Buganda which, by 1954, had been moved to Kibuli, near Kampala. But because up to 1950 few Muslim children had completed Primary Six, in order to join this teacher training school, the number of Muslim teachers available to teach in the Muslim primary schools in this denominational educational era was small. The result was that the Muslim authorities on a number of occasions, employed teachers dismissed by either the Catholic or the Protestant educational organisations. These teachers sometimes, were not particularly good. This affected some Muslim schools especially as far as the Primary Leaving Examination was concerned. This also affected the chances of some Muslim children regarding joining secondary schools and other post-primary institutions.

The situation was improved by local governments during the 1950s, which set up a number of non-denominational primary schools that employed competent teachers trained in Christian denominational teacher training colleges, and were open to all children. Muslims joined these local government schools both primary and junior secondary schools in good numbers. Meanwhile, Kibuli Muslim Junior Secondary School made progress by becoming a double stream school in 1952. The non-denominational secondary schools which Governor Sir Andrew Cohen ordered to be built in the four regions of Uganda, and run by government on non-denominational basis, made secondary education more accessible to Muslim children soon after 1953.

An event which greatly affected the development of Muslim education was the formation of the Uganda Muslim Education Association (UMEA) in 1950, with an African Ugandan as its secretary-general. The Uganda Muslim Education Association was told to develop Muslim education on the same lines as those of the education secretaries-general for the Roman Catholic Mission and for the Native Anglican Church. Through the efforts of tireless Muslim leaders like Mr. R.K. Gava until 1964 the secretary-general, there grew considerable enthusiasm among Uganda Muslims towards secular education for their children which now had an officer in charge. Assisted by the education department, the association re-organised existing Muslim schools, and caused new ones to be started so that by the end of 1952, there were 56 Muslim primary schools in Uganda with 4,379 boys and 1,184 girls on the register. There were 2 junior secondary schools with 128 boys and 4 girls enrolled.

In view of the belated start, the development of education for Muslim children was remarkable. In the year ended 31 December 1960, UMEA had 231 primary schools with an enrolment of 23,986 pupils and 10 junior secondary schools attended by 905 pupils, under its charge. There was in that year no Muslim senior secondary school as such, despite facilities being available at government non-denominational senior secondary schools. The above quoted statistics need not cause alarm form if looked at with reference to the Muslim population. They really mark unquestionably commendable progress. The only note of distress is the absence of a Muslim founded senior secondary school by the end of 1960.

15

Teachers Struggle to Better their Position

The unsatisfactory, undefined conditions of service under which teachers served made them feel the need for teachers' association. The first attempt to form such an association was made by a small group of teachers working at Nabumali High School near Mbale in 1942 when they formed what they called the African School Teachers Association (ASTA) Unfortunately, the first teachers to organise this body and those who joined it subsequently were all Protestants and other teachers in that area from the Roman Catholic group were reluctant to join it. However, this did not stop the association from functioning. Members still hoped that the differences which prevented the Catholics from joining them would disappear if benefits could be gained as a result of the activities of their organisation.

The example of the teachers in Mbale was followed by those around Kampala in 1944 who began in a metropolitan area, and had a great deal of support from those who had little interest in such impediments as tribal and denominational differences. Their organisation, to which they gave the name of the Uganda African Teachers Association (UATA) had from the very beginning a large number of teachers. They maintained that if you were an African teacher you were a teacher whatever area of Uganda you accidentally happened to come and irrespective of your religious belief. The crucial question of the day was how to better teachers' salaries, conditions of service and the self re-education.

Soon UATA made a constitution, which was to guide members in tackling problems that faced them. The constitution was published in 1945 and its main articles were as follows:

- To unite all teachers in Uganda.
- To promote and maintain the interests of the teaching profession and to safeguard the interests and welfare of its members.
- To render the teaching profession attractive to the rising generation of Uganda.
- To secure the solidarity of teachers and extend the influence of the teaching profession.
- To affiliate with local, national and international bodies connected with or interested in the education of the child.
- To maintain a high standard of qualifications, to raise the status of the teaching profession, and to ensure that all the posts in the educational services of the country are open to members.

- To provide means for the co-operation of teachers and the expression of their collective opinion upon matters affecting the interest of education and the teaching profession.
- To enable members to receive fair treatment in whatever part of Uganda they may be and under whatever institution they may be working.
- To associate with or assist the promotion of mass literacy, adult education and the education of the handicapped.
- To purchase, lease property, alter and maintain any building required for the association.
- To hold debates, lectures, talks and election competitions with a view to promoting and advancing the educational, cultural and literary faculties of the members.
- To make presentations to the government and local authorities to invoke their aid for safeguarding and promoting the moral, social and economic life of the members.
- To watch the administration of pension regulations and to endeavour to secure their amendment where necessary.
- To assist an undertaking or company providing or about to provide life assurance for the benefit of members.
- To secure, promote and maintain Teachers' Benevolent and Orphan Fund.

Armed with such a forward looking constitution the leaders of UATA toured the country asking other teachers to join them in an effort to bring pressure to bear on both the government and the missionaries. As a result, they got many teachers to join regardless of their ethnic group and denominational affixations.

Although the government had accepted and welcomed the formation of UATA, the missions, which actually controlled the schools, did everything they could to block it from getting established with many members in their schools. They were very suspicious of its motives. They felt that if teachers belonged to one body they would become military and consequently would be more difficult to control. But the more the missions objected to UATA, the more the teachers came forward to register as members, for they felt that the unsatisfactory salaries and conditions of service could be improved only by joint action of all teachers as members of the association.

To counteract the influence of UATA the missions started denominational teachers' organisation whose members were required to submit to the wishes of the church authorities under which they served. The Catholic Teachers' Guild (CTG) began in this way in the 1940s in the Rubaga Diocese and it has for a long time existed under the name of *Agali Awamu,* (Luganda) implying the solidarity of Catholic teachers and church leaders. Its aim was to discover how best the two groups could co-operate to improve Catholic education. The guild still exists today and claims to promote the social welfare or its members. But it has never involved itself in bargaining with the employers about the rights and privileges of its members. During the vital days of the struggle for the improvement of the teachers' conditions of service and their salaries, the Catholic hierarchy used its influence to see that teachers who supported this point of view led the different branches of the guild in the various parts of Uganda. This only helped to drive the more militant teachers into the ranks of the Uganda Teachers

Association. The Catholic hierarchy allowed Catholic teachers to join it in the end although they were still required to continue their membership of the Catholic Teachers' Guild.

Although the Uganda African Teachers Association claimed to be the teachers' organisation for the whole of Uganda, this was not true until about 1953. Before then its members were mainly teachers from the Buganda area. The association in Mbale continued to operate until 1953 when it was voluntarily dissolved and its members joined the Uganda African Teachers Association since its leaders saw no benefit of operating two separate organisations with the same objectives and interests.

After 1953, the development of the association was for some years slowed down by disharmony between some teachers teaching in primary schools and in what were known as junior schools, on one side, and those teaching in senior secondary schools and teacher training colleges, on the other. The former group of teachers felt that was leadership of the association was concentrated too much in the hands of the latter group. They also feel that their interests and grievances were not being taken seriously and adequately made known to the government. As a matter of fact, Makerere teachers and teachers educated abroad and who were teaching in both teachers colleges and senior secondary schools, tended to occupy all the key posts in the association.

In addition to this they had relatively good salaries, good houses in boarding schools and had other ancillary benefits which were not available to primary and Junior Secondary teachers who were nevertheless in the majority. There was doubt among them as to whether such well-off people were likely to press hard enough for the needs of their lower paid colleagues. Primary school and junior secondary school wanted, apart from better salaries, loans to at least buy motor cycles, and accommodation .

The discord grew worse and worse until the primary and junior secondary school teachers pulled out of the association in 1956 and subsequently registered the Vernacular Primary and Junior Teachers Union (VPJU). Both the union's title and its constitution, which will not appear here, left no room for any other grade of teachers above the junior secondary teachers to join. In 1965 it changed its name to the Uganda Teachers' Union to try to attract teachers above that grade and thus look less sectional.

Whilst UATA and the VPJU had very similar objectives, each organisation interpreted its objectives differently. UATA and later on UTU said that it existed for its members and so its obligations were focused on members only – after all if members were happy the pupils would also gain because the teachers' morale would be high and they would thus be able to care for them better.

The Uganda Teachers Union had quite a big following for the first few years after it had broken away from the Uganda Teachers Association but its membership dropped throughout the 1960s. It considered merging with the

Uganda Teachers Association in 1967 but agreement could not be reached between the two organisations.

The authorities, however, have publicly announced that they are unable to recognise the Uganda Teachers Union because its approach to education is not professional. It behaves like a trade union which may even call on its members to stage strikes. Thus the Uganda Teachers Union has found it difficult to operate without formal government support and it has been gradually losing members. However, it still exists and makes its vague presence felt through very short and occasional press releases and circulars sent to schools and this usually happens as a retaliation to public discussion held by the secretariat of UTA.

Despite the split in 1956, however, the Uganda African Teachers Association, and now the Uganda Teachers Association, grew steadily gaining more and more members even from the splinter groups, who now realised that the solution of their problems was to be militant only within the mother Association. After 1957 offices began to be shared without bias towards a particular section of the educational system, and depended on qualities of leadership alone. Having changed its name to Uganda Teachers Association, in 1962, UTA re-organised itself to operate more effectively and to reach teachers more quickly in all corners of Uganda. It set up a secretariat headed by a permanent secretary. Today two thirds of all the teachers in Uganda belong to it and as a result of teachers coming together in one strong organisation they have achieved many good things. The following are some of the achievements that have been gained since the teachers formed their organisation:-

1. Teachers' salaries have improved considerably since 1940 and a pension scheme was drawn up after a long struggle.
2. Teachers, through their organisation, are represented on educational committees and school boards and on the Teaching Service Commission and the Salaries Advisory Committee.
3. Teachers can go for refresher courses organised and run by their organisation.
4. Conditions of service have improved and are still improving.
5. Teachers have an employer now after almost 20 years of hard fighting for it.
6. Teachers have learnt to save by buying insurance policies through their own scheme and by being encouraged to join credit unions.
7. Teachers in Uganda are consulted by the Government on education matters through their own organisation.
8. Their organisation has put up a very impressive building in Kampala and has built up a good library service in that building which helps teachers to improve their academic and professional abilities.

Notes
1. Thomas Jesse Jones, 1925, *Education in East Africa,* London: Edinburgh House Press.
2. CMS 1922 *Gleaner.*
3. CMS 1928 *News.*
4. Uganda Education Department Annual Report 1933, government Printer Entebbe.
5. Uganda Education Department Annual Report 1937, Government Printer Entebbe.
6. Uganda Education Department Annual Report 1959, Government Printer Entebbe.
7. Uganda Education Department Annual Report 1953, Government Printer Entebbe.
8. Director of Education Annual Report 1957.

PART THREE

DEVELOPMENT OF EDUCATION IN TANGANYIKA 1900-1961

16

From German Administration Days to the Dar-es-Salaam Education Conference 1900-1925

The German Education System and its Objectives

By 1914, the German administration had attempted, as much as it could, to establish a fairly extensive system of education for Africans. At the beginning of 1914, German East Africa had 89 elementary schools and 10 higher schools with an enrolment of about 8,494 pupils. Most of the educational work of the German administration was confined to the coastal area, with Tanga as the main centre.

The educational system set up by the Germans had at least three main objectives. First, it was meant to give training to selected Africans so that they could understand and pass on instructions in writing. Pupils who displayed promise were sent from the elementary school to the nearest higher school usually under a European headmaster where they were taught German. Those who successfully completed the course, which lasted three to four years, would then go to Tanga to be trained as teachers or for a course of advanced studies. Secondly, it emphasised the importance and need for vocational training and practical work. Thirdly, it was to be used to prepare the "native boy" for minor and low-pay jobs so as to reduce the German administration's costs. There was an elementary course in Kiswahili, covering the three Rs, Geography and Hygiene, besides some husbandry. Seeds were provided for school crops, and ploughing was introduced at one school. In Dar-es-Salaam and in Bukoba, three-year primary courses were started with instruction in English, as training for clerical posts.

Again, at Dar-es-Salaam, the government set up a centre for re-training former teachers adding new recruits as well. The training centre was later transferred to Mpwapwa. Meanwhile the main educating force in the country – the missions, were also after recovery from the war shocks, active in the field of education. However, there was no co-operation between them either in policy or matters of finance. Many of the mission schools continued for sometime to give little secular education other than religious instructions. But in 1923 at Minaki, 27 kilometres from Dar-es-Salaam, the UMCA. Mission had established a teacher training college known as St. Andrew's which was soon regarded as the most efficient college in the territory.

The 1924 Phelps-Stocks Commission Reports on Education in Tanganyika

The government's efforts to re-organise the schools in the difficult post-war period were noted by the commission which also noted that a genuine effort had been made to relate the school work to the condition and needs of the people, especially as regards health and agriculture. By the year 1924 government had 74 schools offering primary courses with instructions in Agriculture, Craftwork and Hygiene. The commission however, expressed concern over government's reluctance to assist mission schools. They had this to say:

> The serious departure of Tanganyika from the education policy in British colonies in Africa is in the refusal to give grants-in-aid to mission schools. The government has thus disregarded the most potent ally available in Africa.

The commission urged the government to change its policy and proposed immediate payment of grants-in-aid for mission schools of approved standard, and further called for close co-operation between government and missions in the area of education. The commission strongly advised:

(a) use of common nomenclature of types of schools and classes,
   a common language policy.
(b) appointment of more education officers to supervise both mission and government schools.
(c) establishment of an advisory committee on African education,
(d) government to take a lead in setting up different types of schools in various parts of the country.

The report had some impact on the development of education in the period beginning 1925.

Government Accepts Responsibility for Secular Education.

Up to 1925, the Tanganyika Government accepted responsibility only for schools organised and run at government expense. However, following the publication of a White Paper called "Education Policy in British Tropical Africa", and the Phelps-Stokes report, this policy was revised soon after 1925. The government accepted as its obligation to guide secular education, to make financial provision and to ascertain whether there was a uniform system and standard of efficiency.

As a first step, the Governor, Sir Donald Cameron invited representatives of voluntary educational agencies to the first Education conference with government representatives to discuss, among other things, how government and missionaries might co-operate in task of giving Tanganyika suitable education. The conference, which lasted from October 5 to 12 October 1925, was an important landmark in the history of education in Tanganyika.

The Director of Education Presents a Plan for the Organisation and Control of Education 1925

The director of education, at this conference, presented and had discussed a memorandum on "Suggested Organisation of a System of Grants-in-Aid, to assisted Schools".

The memorandum, which was nothing else but an official plan for organising and controlling education, was warmly received by the conference. The government, it was indicated, would pay grants-in-aid to recognised types of schools, which were listed as:

(a) teachers training schools
(b) girls boarding schools and schools for infant – welfare training
(c) central schools
(d) industrial schools
(e) elementary or village schools
(f) holiday schools

Each type of school was clearly defined and the amount of grant to be paid was indicated.. The idea of setting up a general advisory committee on education was cordially received and no one at the conference, it seems, found the duties assigned to the committee, unacceptable or excessive. The committee was briefly to be charged with the following duties:

(a) Submitting to the governor for his approval, an education policy for the whole of Tanganyika Territory and considering any changes of that policy as circumstances necessitated them.

(b) Deciding and recommending syllabuses of instruction and what books to use in the school.

(c) Appointment of examiners, and itself forming the Board of Examinations for all public examinations.

(d) Finding out what books were urgently required in the schools, get them written and published, and to encourage the publication of literature in Kiswahili. It was also proposed to set up District Advisory Committee on Education, with Provincial Commissioners as chairmen and care being taken to make sure Africans were members.

Mission Schools Under Government Supervision

The scheme of organisation, as indicated in the director's memorandum, brought all mission schools under supervision through a government superintendent. Although it was stressed that his duty would be to foster friendly relations with missions, it seems he was going to be the medium through which it was planned to control and insist on the standard of efficiency that would be required of mission schools. The director of education made it quite clear when replying to some of the questions raised in the course of the discussion on his paper, that it would be the inspectors who would decide whether a school measured up to the standard of efficiency required or not. A satisfactory report on the behaviour of the pupils, their learning ability and keenness in all subjects, work in the school garden included, would be the criterion rather than examination results. It was further made clear that whether a school was aided or not, it would be liable to government inspection any time, to ensure efficiency.

The missions were given a free hand in deciding whether to admit or not , pupils of other creeds into their schools. But it was stated clearly that where pupils of another creed were admitted, they should not be compelled to go to classes for religious instruction.

17

Development in Education after the 1925 Dar-es-Salaam Conference up to 1939

Legislative Council's Interest in Education

From 1926 the Tanganyika Legislative Council members began to show and express keen interest in the department of education's work and indicated the developments they wanted to be carried out.

At the December 1926 meeting, for instance, concern was expressed over the meagerness of what government proposed to spend on education in the following financial year. When it was noticed that only 3 per cent of the budget of the territory was all that would be spent on education, members urged the director of education to ask for a large sum of money in the near future so as to meet liberally the requirements of his department.

Fear was also expressed that if care was not exercised schools might overproduce partially trained clerks at the expense of agricultural and technical education. Some members felt that there was already a surplus of *karanis* but a scarcity of trained artisans. It was suggested that all schools which had received grants from the government clerks should be required to include instruction in agriculture, in their programme. However, as the director of education explained in his attempt to allay anxiety expressed over educational institutions being given a clerical bias, his department, moving cautiously and slowly, was giving due attention to industrial training. His department, he told the council, had plans to mount a system of apprenticeship to departments. It was already insisting on every village school having a garden or a plantation where all pupils would be practically taught simple agriculture.

Two main developments which practically attempted to ensure education had the practical element and relevance that the Legislative Council members were calling for. They were: (a) the native administration school movement and, (b) central schools
The developments will now be discussed briefly.

1. The Native Administration Schools Movements

The rise of native administration schools was soon after 1926. Sir Donald Cameron, Governor of Tanganyika (1925 – 31), was a firm believer in a system known as "indirect rule", which meant in brief, devolution of authority for local government to traditional authorities such as chiefs, or councils of elders, or groups of people whom Tanganyikans had recognised as tribal authorities before colonial times.

In 1926, Governor Cameron enacted the Native Authority Ordinance, which gave local authorities a number of tasks among which, implicitly, was the building of schools for their own people. The chiefs displayed considerable enthusiasm for this and great many native administration schools were built using some money from their treasuries. This boosted self-help.

While they followed government syllabus, the aim of all native administration schools was to provide practical education to prepare pupils to lie in their villages. They all kept gardens and even coffee plantations, for instance, in Kilimanjaro areas. Some of them were boarding schools while others were day schools.

The education department report for the year ended 31 December 1929, gives an interesting account of the development of two native administration schools in Mwanza Province, and the account goes a long way in indicating what these schools were like. The report says:

> The most important developments of the year have been the opening of two Native Authority schools in the Mazwa and Kwimba Districts and a new town school in Mwanza. The first, Binza School, named after the local division of the tribe, was opened at Shanwa, the District headquarters, on 7th January. This school opened with 118 boys, of whom about 100 were boarders, the latter consisting almost entirely of the sons of headmen and minor chiefs. Four teachers were posted. The boarding accommodation consists of three "villages", each with six boys' houses, a teacher's house and a refectory and its own kitchen, so that each is a self-contained entity and its boys come from one area of the District. The classrooms are built some three or four hundred yards from the "villages".

> The boys work on the Native Administration farm, a large portion of which is set aside for the growing of food crops for the school. In a school of this type a considerable portion of school time is set aside for agricultural work, more especially during the rainy season. Drill is under the control of a drill instructor, who is an ex-K.A.R. sergeant, and who under the head teacher largely has charge of discipline out of school hours. All boarders are clothed and boarded free at the expense of the Native Administration. Levying of fees has purposely been avoided up to the present till the results of education become more apparent to the parents of the boys and they can appreciate their value. The average headman, too, cannot afford to pay for his son's education. The general work and organization in the school throughout the year has reached a very high level.

> The Kwimba Native Administration school at Ngudu, the District Headquarters, was opened on 11th February with eighty-one boys, the great majority of whom were again sons of headmen and minor chiefs. Two teachers were posted, and

later on ex-K.A.R. Corporal as drill instructor. The general layout and organisation of the school has been very much the same as at Maswa, though classrooms and villages are closer together. The introduction of Shs. 4/- per month boarding fees at the beginning of the September term resulted in fifteen boys being removed by their parents owing to inability to pay. It is hoped to reduce fees to Shs. 2/- as from 1ˢᵗ January and to raise the number of pupils. A third teacher was posted at the beginning of December.[1]

Generally, in the native administration schools, there was great enthusiasm for "tribal education" especially as many sons of chiefs attended, who would later be responsible men in he district. In Bukoba, for instance, the chiefs enthusiastically financed schools which could recapture some of the old tribal lore which had been taught in the "bakama" or chiefs' schools of German and pre-German days.

In another area, the district officer procured the services of an elder of high repute to visit his native administration school twice a week to teach boys tribal history and customs. These lessons were copied down in Kiswahili by a teacher to form a useful collection.

As one talks about native administration schools it is difficult to avoid talking briefly about the school started by Chief Towegale in Ulanga District. It began as a simple school to train the sons of headmen "in what a headman should know." By the middle 1930s it had grown into a boarding school of about 40 pupils, aged from four to 14, who had first of all to grow food. The timetable was drawn up in such a way that pupils worked in the garden for four hours a day. Besides the teaching of the three Rs, and Agriculture, Kiswahili, tribal history, singing, dancing and etiquette were taught to ensure that school-leavers had some real usefulness to the tribe. Supervision was by a board of four elders, who took it in turns to inspect the outdoor work every day and report to the chief. Education authorities impressed by this school wrote: "The school is in the centre of the village and is the centre of village life. It has already undertaken far-reaching agricultural experiments, and is profoundly influencing methods of cultivation".

Normally, the native administration paid for the building of its schools, and for equipment provided by the education department, which also recruited the teachers, only a very small proportion of whom where certificated in the early years. Quite often, under the enthusiastic patronage of chiefs, these schools became boarding or semi-boarding schools, with strict discipline aimed at training future administrators. They carried out interesting experiments in teaching about administration. For example, Ndomo School which opened in 1928, taught the principles of native administration both by formal lessons and through the organisation of the school itself.

A school court with a local chief as president tried offences, against conduct and discipline once a week and the procedure was an exact replica of that of the native courts of the district. Generally speaking, the idea was making these schools, and indeed all village schools, the cultural centres of village life, and to emphasise the need for sound practical training whereby local life would benefit. However, that these schools were seen by many largely as a stepping stone to the higher and literary forms of education offered in the central schools, is beyond doubt.

2. Central Schools

The government, through its department of education, attached considerable importance to central schools and clearly indicated what they were and what they were expected to stress in their programmes in the statement.

The central school is what the title indicates, a centre of all activities, where the carpenter or blacksmith is just as good and often better than boys in the upper English classes; and it is surely a healthy corrective to budding clerical priggishness that it may subject to robust industrial discipline[2]

A central school firstly, provided for four further classes of primary education with English as the medium of instruction, and awarded what was called the Central School Leaving Certificate to those who passed a public examination conducted by the education department assisted by missionaries. Secondly, central schools admitted industrial apprentices of Standard 2 level of education and indented them for four years. The aim on the industrial side was to produce a "literate artisan," who took a four-year apprenticeship course, such as carpentry, metal-working or printing at Dar-es-Salaam; telegraphy or hospital dressing at Tanga; and agricultural course at the inland schools, or a commercial course at Tabora.

There was a free set of tools for each successful apprentice at the end of this course. The idea of a central school came largely from the Government, but the missions too adopted it, and by 1930 the UMCA, CMS, the Bielfield Mission, the Italian Fathers of the Consulate, the Fathers of the Holy Ghost, the White Fathers, the Swiss Benedictine Fathers, the Moravians and the Methodists all had them. They offered various type of industrial training as well as literary and religious education. Government circles believed that these mission schools gave a moral training, which the government central schools to a certain degree lacked. Efforts were therefore made to supply to government, central schools the moral code and training in ethical standards which it was felt went with a Western type of education, especially when the new idea cut across tribal usages and tribal authority. Thus the missionaries, and also the Koranic teachers, were called in to instruct the government central school boys in their respective faiths.

A number of central schools appear to have been successful. The Central School of Tanga, for instance, was reported on well by the Department of Education in its annual report for 1929. Of the school, the report said:

There were about 400 boys in the school, of whom roughly eighty-five per cent are day boys. The average percentage of attendance during 1929 was just under ninety-six per cent, as compared with ninety-one per cent - for the previous year. When compared with the early years of the school's existence since re-organisation began, the achievement is a striking testimony to the position it holds in the estimation of the people, more particularly as it has been attained under the enervating influence other than moral persuasion and the knowledge that the "slacker" will have to make room for another who is keen. A very significant fact is that these, for the tropics, very remarkable figures, would have been impossible without the assistance of the Medical Department, and they prove conclusively that the general standard of health of the children of the township has been definitely raised as a result of the careful medical attention they receive at school.

During the year eleven pupils were presented for the Central Schools Certificates, eight of whom were successful. During the same period thirty-four industrial certificates were issued to boys who had successfully completed their industrial training, all of whom, so far as the Headmaster knows, have found employment.

At the end of December there were eighty-eight boys in the English standards, thirty-five apprenticed to telegraphy - mostly for the railways - whom were also receiving instruction in English, and eighty-nine apprenticed to industries, including five as hospital dresses. In view of the fact that it is usual for some boys to transfer from Standard III (first year in English), in which there were forty pupils, to industries, the industrial position may be looked upon as eminently satisfactory been arranged that the school will recruit ten apprentices annually for the Traffic Department of the Railways.[3]

Government Takes Definite Legal Steps to Control and Supervise Education in all the Territory

The 1927 African Education Ordinance
Two years after the 1925 Education Conference, on 31st March 1927, the governor and the Legislative Council, enacted the African Education ordinance 1927. The ordinance embodied the contents of the memorandum the director of education had discussed at the conference.

The ordinance required all schools and all teachers to be registered with the director of education. For teaching in any government, or any assisted school, registration was compulsory. No school may be opened or maintained by any person unless registered six months after the commencement of the ordinance. The director of education was empowered to forbid use of any textbook or materials which, in his opinion, were not up to the expected standard. He or his representative could close a school which, according to the evidence obtainable, was conducted in contravention of the ordinance. The director for other officials of the government listed in the ordinance, were authorised to enter any school, at any reasonable time, examine records, and sit in class to hear what was going on. According to the same ordinance, the director had authority to open up schools anywhere he though fit.

Reaction to the 1927 Education Ordinance

The missionaries did not welcome the ordinance whose previsions they thought diverged from what had been agreed upon at the Dar-es-Salaam conference in October 1925. They were not happy to learn among other things, that:

(a) all schools shall be under government supervision and control.
(b) instruction was to be, even in the bush schools, exclusively in the Kiswahili language.
(c) religious instruction was according to the letter of the law to be given outside the regular schools hours;
(d) the medium of instruction in central schools was to be English.
(e) To teach in a government or an aided school one must be registered as Grade 1 or Grade 2 teacher or must be on the provisional list.

In a conference held at Maranga from 20 - 26 September 1928, representatives of missionary groups after a long discussion addressed the following requests to the government:-

(a) Religious instruction in all schools be given a central place since it was the chief means of character building.
(b) Bush schools be maintained and opened without being registered.
(c) Instruction in the first years be in the vernacular but Kiswahili become the medium of instruction in later years.
(d) Teachers of vernacular schools be trained in Kiswahili to that they might very well understand the subjects of the course to be able to teach intelligently.
(e) The medium of instruction in the central schools be Kiswahili.

There was a good deal of discussion between the missions and government in England and in Tanganyika. However, the government indicated to the missionaries that,

(a) East Africa education would soon follow the Western African pattern and that the line government was taking was the correct one.
(b) The Tanganyikans were not on the side of the missions, but on that of the government. They wanted as much English and high standards as were within reach. They wanted full partnership in Western civilisation.

The controversy continued with missions convinced that educational wisdom was on their side while the government maintained the provisions of the ordinance would cause education for Africans to develop on the right lines. Unfortunately, the coming of the World Great Depression in 1929 - 33, so severely affected the government's revenue that mission objections aside, there were no funds to implement the ordinance.

The Education System in 1928

The education system for which the ordinance of 1927 was made consisted of the following:-

1. Elementary (vernacular) schools the category to which the following institutions belonged:
   (a) Unassisted mission schools staffed by uncertificated teachers giving only catechetical instruction.
   (b) Assisted mission schools (village schools and vernacular sections of central schools) - instruction based on syllabus and given by certificated teachers.
   (c) Government village schools with day pupils only admitted and run by qualified teachers.
   (d) Native administration schools (already fully described in this account).

2. Middle schools
   These central schools with standard VI as the top and providing a course leading to the Central School Leaving Certificate. There was no secondary education given at this time. Tabora had a clerical course for boys intended mainly for the African civil service. Mpwapwa had a teacher training college and so had Minaki.

Further Education Ordinances and Regulations Tighten Government Control over Schools and Teachers

The amending the African Education Ordinance No. 24 of 1936, in conjunction with the Registration of Schools and Teacher Regulations 1937, further tightened government control over schools and teachers. The ordinance gave a new and exclusive definition to the school which was not defined as an institution at which African pupils attended a regular course of secular instruction, and included training institutions. The ordinance would not have catechetical centres, theological institutions and seminars, call themselves schools. The regulations defined a teacher afresh. To be registered, one had to be a graduate, a holder of a diploma or certificate considered adequate by the director of education. Alternatively, holding one of the 3 territorial certificates namely, Grade I (English), Grade II (vernacular) and Women Teachers Certificate, would make a teacher eligible for registration. Not everybody feeling like doing so, was going to teach.

What Were the Aims of Education After 1927 Education Ordinance?

After the enactment of the ordinance, greatly increased provision was made for education. The work of the education department expanded rapidly. There was an increase in staff at the headquarters, and expenditure on education rose from Shs. 360,000 in 1925 to Shs. 2,440,000 in 1931.

From the above quoted figures, which may appear to us now to represent a small sum of money, but which actually represented a considerable amount of money in the period under review, it is not out of place to ask this question. Why was the government spending so much money on education? What did educators want Tanganyika to get from schooling? To answer this question we have to go back to the White Paper of 1925, already mentioned in this account. That White Paper which, as you have already read, was titled "Education Policy in British Tropical Africa", entrusted to the Tanganyika Government the responsibility of producing capable, trustworthy and public-spirited leaders for Tanganyika, of producing trained men to man posts in the administrative and technical services. The government was also charged with the responsibility of raising the standard and welfare of the community as a whole, by raising the efficiency of the greatest number of Tanganyikans possible. The government was to make sure that no gulf developed between those who had been to school and the rest of the community.

It was, therefore, resources permitting, intended to carry out this mission. At best, those engaged in educational activities tried to train and fit pupils when they left school, to live in a world wider than their forefathers had known, a world of hitherto unknown complexity, money economy, easier inter-regional communications and secular and foreign authority superior to local authority, a world of large numbers of aliens whom he would have to work for or work with.

It is one thing to state the aims of education boldly, liberally, and in language that make them unquestionably noble, and another to draw up a programme that makes it possible for the aims to be achieved or not. It is more often than not difficult to determine whether certain aims announced have been achieved or not. If the aim is to increase enrolment, that this has been achieved, is easily determined. But when for instance, can one say with certainty that public - spirited leaders have been produced? What is the yardstick for public-spirited leadership? Who decides Mr. X is public-spirited? These are some of the questions that are possible to ask.

What was taught?

To the best of their ability those charged with the task of directing education in Tanganyika, tried to draw up a curriculum which they thought would make it possible to achieve some of the more attainable of the aims states. The curriculum, in addition to purely academic subjects, included subjects with a very pronounced practical element. The education department's curriculum contained a rural industries course for schools, with carpentry where emphasis was placed on making agricultural implements such as hoe-handles, ox-yokes, ox-ploughs and on building and improving cattle kraals, and on making stools, beds, mortars and furniture from simple materials. The curriculum included smithery, a course in which pupils learnt to forge and weld, soldering and riveting, and carrying out bicycle repairs.

The period of rapid expansion was brought to an abrupt end by the great Economic Depression of 1929 - 33 which hit Tanganyika, as it did to many parts of the world, very severely. Industrial schools in Bukoba, Mpwapwa, Moshi and Mwanza were shut down and staff drastically reduced. Recovery from the bad times did not come until about 1936, but then it lasted only three years and the Second World War began, making it very difficult to undertake further expansion.

The Issue of Using English or Kiswahili

There was a lively debate in the Legislative Council meeting of June 1939 on what language should be taught and used in Tanganyika schools. Major G.L.O. Grundy moved a motion requesting the government to consider immediately the adoption of English as the lingua franca of the territory, and thus obviously the language to be taught in schools. He forcibly argued that Africans wanted English and that the majority of East Africans were demanding its use. He quoted Uganda as an example here Kiswahili had been rejected to be spoken or to be taught in schools, and where therefore, English and vernacular languages were taught. The Kikuyu of Kenya, he further contended, had also opposed Kiswahili. Grundy further told the council that the Africans of Kenya, Uganda, and Tanganyika were not asking for English in order to become clerks, but in order to have a broader knowledge of things.

The next speaker, who was the director of education and who fully supported the teaching and use of English in schools emphasised the importance and necessity of seeing to it that it was properly and thoroughly well taught.

The director of medical services, while able to inform the council from his experience as a teacher of sanitary inspectors, whose course had been conducted in Kiswahili that the Kiswahili was a growing language, supported the motion. However he, like the director of education, wanted to see English well taught.

Another speaker, expressed fear that teaching Tanganyikans English would lay them open to following agitators. They would pick up objectionable politics from reading newspapers from other countries. If at all it became necessary to teach English, he continued, the government should go very slowly about it. He was briefly saying that for political reasons English should not be taught. Yet another speaker argued that if Africans were taught English, they would not go back to the land to do agriculture.

One Major Grundy, refuting all these naïve arguments, said that if the African wanted to become a clerk or refused to return to the land, or he followed agitators, it would not be because he had been taught English, but simply because the system of education was faulty. The governor in his concluding remarks on this debate, saw no political danger in encouraging the teaching of English in schools. He indicated that the government would do its utmost to promote the teaching and use of English in the territory.

Kiswahili was not removed from schools but it was only used as the medium of instruction in the lower classes of the school system that is standard 1-4.

18

The Isherwood Committee Probes: Two Questions Raised in 1939 Concerning Education Developments up to 1960

The two questions raised were:
1. How adequate were the educational facilities available to the Tanganyikans?
2. What were the educational requirements of European and Indian communities?

The governor, on 31st March, 1939, appointed a committee under the chairmanship of Mr. A. A. M. Isherwood, O.B.E., then director of education, to probe these questions, report back their findings, and also come forward with proposals and recommendations.

It would seem odd to us now, that it should have been necessary to raise the second question. However, in the period under review, and indeed until Tanganyika gained her independence in 1961, the administration operated three separate schools: one for Europeans, for Indians and for Africans. And it is no exaggeration to suggest that often facilities at African schools were not like those at Europeans and Indian schools. It would probably sound difficult for us now to appreciate the fact that the educational requirements of the Indian community, for instance, who were in Tanganyika to stay, should have been regarded to be different from those of Tanganyikans. In 1939, however, it was acceptable to the people.

The committee which consisted of 18 members including two Africans, one of whom was Martin Kayamba M.B.E., spent no less than six months at the job. In the course of their enquiry, they found that of the 480,000 boys of school-going age in the territory, only 53,798 attended school. Of the 520,000 females of school going age, only 22,560 were at school in 1939. They also presented the following pattern concerning providing education:-

Education Body	Boys	%	Girls	%
Government	6,121	11.4	717	3.1
Native Administration	3,671	6.8	55	0.1
Aided Voluntary Agencies	17,387	32.3	7,935	35.1
Unaided Voluntary Agencies	26,619	49.5	13,853	61.5

Those facilities for the education of Africans were inadequate, in an inescapable conclusion from the recommendations made by the committee.

Recommendations of the Committee

While suggesting no radical alteration of the educational system as it was then, the committee recommended considerable development. They recommended strongly a very great expansion of primary school facilities to be undertaken. As more and more teachers became available, the committee recommended opening up a large number of village day schools which, they held, would provide the foundation for the territory's education system. More little stress was put on the establishment of a rural educational system under which a pupil would move from a village school to a middle school serving several villages and from there to a provincial teacher or industrial training centre which they wanted to see situated near a veterinary department or a hospital or a native administration headquarters. They also wanted such a school to be staffed by a European Headmaster, an industrial instructor and selected African teachers.

It was hoped that the majority of pupils who attended middle schools would return to their villages, to form an educated citizenry with interest in Agriculture. The committee recommended that primary education and teacher training be organised on a provincial basis and that salary scales of teachers be revised to suit each province. Provision of respectable housing for teachers was strongly recommended because, it was argued, the manner and the surroundings in which the teacher lived, should be an example to the neighbourhood.

Disturbed by the ill-disciplined tendencies of some youths in Dar-es-Salaam, the committee whole-heartedly advocated plans to be made to provide compulsory primary education in urban centres, especially in at least 12 largest towns for the territory. For Dar-es-Salaam, the appointment of an African attendance officer and a welfare worker was, in the view of the committee, an urgent matter, that could not be delayed any longer.

That only three per cent of the male population of school going age attended secondary school, did not alarm them. However, they attached weight to the completion of standards 8 to 10 alternatively known as junior secondary. It was felt that 9 government and 14 mission schools would meet the needs of the territory for men with junior secondary education, for a period of ten years. Note that only five junior secondary schools existed then and therefore 18 needed to be up-graded.

It was also recommended that the government schools at Tabora and Tanga, plus a Church of England and Catholic Church schools, be raised to full secondary school status to prepare candidates for Makerere College and Mulago School. The committee looked to Makerere for supplying school masters of a higher grade. On the subject of the training of clerks, committee members suggested successful completion of the Junior secondary course to be a prerequisite, and emphasised a broadened clerical course. It was not felt necessary to establish schools for training Tanganyikans in advanced branches of technical work since Makerere provided it.

Special Recommendations on Female Education

As you should have noticed from the figures of enrolment quoted from their findings, the committee expressed justifiable concern over the sad state of African female education in the territory. Not only was it inadequate in quantity but in quality as well. The explanation for this sad state of affairs was lack of properly qualified African women teachers, and the inefficiency of those available. The committee urged he appointment of women provincial education officers, to take a close interest in girls education. Recruiting European women teachers for Tanganyika was unanimously supported. The problem of girl's education could further be tackled by opening up many primary schools each with a European on staff and with a teacher training section attached.

A curriculum with the usual practical subjects, namely domestic science, household economy, child care, hygiene and gardening, for girls was strongly recommended. To put this into effect, the appointment of an organiser of Domestic Science was advocated. And for the European Community, the committee felt that Tanganyika should concentrate on the establishment of a small number of large schools since the number of pupils to cater for was small. It was recommended that European children should go abroad for secondary school education.

It is surprising that although the committee recommended for Indians an educational system adapted to Tanganyika's needs, it still saw it fit for this to be done in separate racial schools. The ambition of every local Indian education committee that its school prepare pupils for the Junior Cambridge Certificate, was deplored by the committee, as often the staff available had neither the competency nor the qualifications to prepare pupils for the examination. Hence the institution of a local examination was advised.

How Valuable was the Isherwood Education Committee's Report and Recommendations?

Unfortunately, before the committee could submit its report and recommendations, the Second World War broke out on 3 September 1939. The committee was told to go ahead with its work until it was completed in 1940, because it was felt that a review of educational work was urgent at this point, despite difficulties and dislocation as a result of the war.

As you can see, considerable space in this account has been devoted to a mention of the major recommendations of the committee. The main reason for this is that the proposals which were the result of a thorough enquiry into the territory's education were accepted in principle by the Colonial Office in London as a general plan for post-war 1939 - 45, educational expansion. And indeed, the Ten-Year Plan for Development of African education was largely based on the recommendations of the committee.

The Main Developments After the Isherwood Report (1945 - 1960)

The Ten-Year Plan 1947 - 1957

The Ten-Year Plan for the Development of African Education 1947-57 was launched in April 1947. Based, as already mentioned, largely on recommendations of the 1939 Central Education Committee, it provided a total of Shs. 107,837,800 to be spent on education and set out to raise the number of African pupils at school from 118,000 in 1940, to 281,800 in 1956. In 1950 when the plan came up for review, the target was made 310,000 Africans pupils in 1956.

The plan emphasised the expansion of primary school education and no effort was spared in trying to se this materialise. However, the main problems encountered were lack of buildings and teachers to cope with the planned expansion. Two measures proposed by the chief secretary to the government in Dar-es-Salaam were taken to deal with the problems.

1. It was arranged to have pupils of classes one and two to attend school in the afternoon while the pupils of classes three and four attended their lessons in the morning, so that a given number of teachers and classrooms could cope with nearly twice the number of pupils.

2. To increase the number of teachers, students who failed their grade II course could now obtain licences to teach; also the department of education tried to persuade those girls who were completing Primary Six to go into teaching. Attempt was also made to persuade class five girls to go into teaching as well. All these would be licensed to teach. The unfortunate thing about this measure was that it encouraged some people to think that teaching was a job that could be done by anybody whether trained or untrained, or even by those who had failed examinations at any stage. It had an adverse effect on the

status of the teacher. However, as a result of this measure, Tanganyika primary school enrolment increased.

By the end of the Ten-Year Plan, in many places, however, the increase in the supply of primary facilities had actually outstripped the demand for them. For example, in 1958 it was established that 20,000 primary school places remained unfilled. Perhaps this, it seems, might have been due to a high rate of wastage which, obviously, caused non-utilization of the facilities. Wastage was particularly considerable among girls. The magnitude of wastage in primary schools in the period 1947 - 1959 is vividly portrayed in the table below which has been extracted from Annual Summaries of the Department of Education Dar-es-Salaam 1947 - 59.

1947-50 and 1956-59 compared percent drop-out				
Between classes		1-2	Classes 2-3	Classes 3-4
1947-50	Boys	28.0	12.4	12.1
	Girls	39.9	27.8	33.0
1956-59	Boys	10.4	6.5	0.9
	Girls	15.4	14.0	12.21

It is not out of place, at this point, to mention one feature of the Tanganyika education system which was that the bulk of the schools were boarding. In all, except a few densely populated areas such as Tanga, Moshi, and Bukoba, all district schools, middle schools i.e. from primary five to primary eight, especially from 1950 were boarding schools, and so were the secondary schools. The reason for this being that population was sparse in many places so that pupils had to be collected from a large area, involving distances which could not be easily walked daily.

This made education expensive and it tended to remove the young boys and girls from their homes at a relatively early age of their lives, and perhaps made them somewhat unfamiliar with their background especially if such pupils climbed up the academic ladder to university level (this is a highly debated point). Could this have been of the reasons besides cost, why after independence the boarding school system was looked at with much disapproval by those in power and it was suggested that the majority of schools should be day schools.

It was part of the Ten-Year Plan to concentrate full senior secondary education at three centres at first till others were built. It will be recalled that by 1939, Tanganyika had two schools which were offering secondary school education up to class ten, namely Tanga Government School, and Tabora Boy's School. These two were actually junior secondary schools at the end of which boys sat, as they did in Uganda, for the Makerere Entrance Examination. In those days Makerere was no more than an upper part of the secondary school education (without A-level section) and indeed, some of its students sat for the Cambridge School Certificate or London Matriculation there.

There was a high demand for secondary school facilities to be provided in Tanganyika from 1947 onwards because firstly, Makerere College had, after the recommendation of the De La Warr Commission of 1937 and with the influence of Sir Phillip Mitchel the Governor of Uganda then, raised its entry standard. It had become difficult to gain entrance into Makerere without a sound secondary school education background. Secondly, both the central and local governments now wanted to employ boys with good secondary education. Plans to concentrate full senior secondary education at three centres namely, Tabora and Pugu and Minaki does not call for quarrelling with the arrangement. Much as this was inadequate, there were some understandable reasons. First of all, the exams at the end of Primary Four, Primary Six, and Primary Eight and at secondary (junior) severely reduced numbers of the available pupils who would be selected on merit for the full secondary course. Secondly, there was a serious shortage of staff of the calibre required. For these reasons (and perhaps others which would be very difficult to substantiate) the intake for a full secondary course remained very small to justify the immediate turning of other junior secondary schools into full senior secondary schools. The three institutions maintained a high standard and sent good students to Makerere. They were also the pioneers of Higher School Certificate courses in the territory when Makerere started demanding the certificate as sign of academic fitness for admission.

At its review in 1950, the plan made more provision for a girl's education, indicated there was to be an increase in teacher training facilities and that provision would be made for the inspection and supervision of all educational institutions.

Before concluding this section we propose to show in figures the position Tanganyika was in, on the eve regaining her independence. We hope that in the figures will be some indication that the Ten-Year Plan and subsequent plans were executed well and the targets set were achieved.

The Education System by 1957

By 1955 there were three stages of education:

(a) Primary standards 1 - 4. Here emphasis was on the 3 Rs. No English was taught, Kiswahili was used.

(b) Middle school - Standards 5 - 8. These schools replaced what had been known before as 'primary district schools' in 1950 when the ten-year plan was revised. The middle school was specially intended to give a four-year course in English and general education designed in such a way that it prepared promising pupils for further education and also catered for those completing their formal education at standard 8.

As stated in the provisional syllabus published in 1952, every effort, it was so claimed, was made to relate the course of instruction closely to the daily practical life of the community where the school was located.

By 1955, entry to the middle schools, most of which were boarding, was based on success in the competitive and selective examinations set and marked at provincial level. Fees of Shs. 250 a year, were paid towards maintenance and boarding costs. The department of education reported favourably on the progress of middle schools. The practical part of the course, after some initial misgivings on the part of pupils and parents, became acceptable. Practical agriculture was insisted on, and the officials of the department of agriculture in conjunction with the provincial education officer, drew up a scheme in which they tried to make sure that lessons learnt in the classroom could be practically illustrated in the area where the school stood.

(c) Secondary Standard 9 - 12. The terminal point here was the Cambridge School Certificate Examination. By 1955, there were three such institutions one of which was St. Francis College Pugu where Julius K. Nyerere (MA Edinburgh) taught and was one of the first two Africans in Tanganyika to teach at that level.

The Five Year Plan 1957 - 1961

A new Five-Year Plan for African Education for the period 1957-1961 was drawn up in 1956 by the director of education so as to have it available at the beginning of the period it was designed for. There was now widespread demand for a rapid expansion of educational facilities, and the new plan was, as far as it was possible, addressed to this demand.

There were, as the governor in his address to the Legislative Council meeting of 25th April, 1956, indicated, different schools of thought as to what stage of education for Tanganyikans should receive greatest attention in the course of the five-year desired expansion. Some opinion was expressed in favour of having the primary school education expanded, rather than post-primary and secondary education. There was also another view which advocated that all effort be concentrated on the secondary and post-secondary segments of the education ladder. These, it seemed, were two extremes, and a choice between, was not easy to make.

The government preferred to take a middle course and the new plan provided for the consolidation of what had already been done and for a gradual expansion. The plan for example, wanted to strengthen the development of the middle schools already in existence and to expand secondary school education with close regard as to how this expansion fitted into the rest of the structure.

The plan thus took a cautious approach to the question of the demanded educational expansion. It is difficult to have a quarrel with this, just as it would be wrong to suspect an intention to hold those concerned behind. The situation was that there were limiting factors which were briefly but clearly, outlined by the governor when he addressed the council, as already mentioned, in April 1956, namely: (a) The envisaged production of teachers could only be matched with the proposed rate of expansion. (b) Building costs had risen so sharply that it would not be possible to provide accommodation for numbers larger than those the plan envisages. (c) Lack of funds was a major factor. The territory's revenue was not expanding at a high rate and, moreover, there were other departments to finance.

The Five-Year Plan is Criticised

The plan came under severe criticism about one-and-a-half years after its inception. It was felt that the plan had not set out to give nor was it going to give Tanganyika the educational expansion she needed. In the Legislative Council meeting of 13th June, 1958 particularly, dissatisfaction was expressed by Tanganyikan members in no uncertain terms. For example, the problem of the bottleneck at Standard 8 had not been addressed since many deserving students stopped here, because there were no adequate secondary schools to absorb them. It was even suggested that the minister of social services give permission to individuals to open private secondary schools as some people had done in Uganda.

It was further complained that the middle school programme had too much of agricultural bias at the expense of other subjects; and thus did not adequately prepare those who wished to go on for further education at secondary school level. "Was every pupil at a middle school meant to go back to the land?" A concerned member wondered. Technical training facilities provided were inadequate. Lack of provision for nursery schools for Africans in big towns was developed. The absence of provision for a secondary school in Dar-es-Salaam was seriously questioned and the establishment of such a school was strongly urged.'

The government had answers to all these charges as usual. However, the range of items of education over which Tanganyika Council members expressed serious concern, indicated that the new plan did not fully meet Tanganyikas' educational needs. The snag often was that these plans were drawn up without the participation of the people for whom they were meant.

The year when this Five-Year Plan came to an end, was the year Tanganyika gained her independence and we shall shortly have a look at education from 1961. Let us in the next chapter look at some of the criticism that it is possible to level at the pre-independence educational system under British administration particularly.

19

Criticism of the pre-Independence Education System Under British Administration

Three Racial Systems of Education were Allowed to Grow up
First of all, in Tanganyika, as in the other two East African territories under them, the British administration operated or allowed three separate educational systems to be operated on a racial basis. This, it is said, was done for the reason that to develop a unified system would present difficult problems educationally and financially. Educational problems would arise because the members of the three communities had different cultures and languages and financial problems would arise because the different systems were financed from different means. But were these really serious and insurmountable problems? It may be asked.

If history be defined as the story of challenge and response then it is possible to argue that the British administrators were faced by the challenge to provide or to cause to be provided, a system of education for three ethnically different groups in a territory they administered. The territory was first administered under a mandate of the League of Nations and subsequently under the United Nations' trusteeship and this was no easy task, in a country of vast size and very limited financial resources. The colonialists responded to the huge challenge by operating three separate systems which worked well, it could further be argued.

But as many people will agree, a response to a challenge, often depends on a number of forces at work at the material time. Some of these forces may be financial, some may be political, and yet some may be purely subjective and attitudinal. If this line of argument is accepted, then, it is possible to hazard a suggestion that, in circumstances when the tendency was to rank in a descending order the people who lived in East Africa, from Europeans, the Indians and others, then lastly the Africans at the bottom, it is no wonder that having put the three groups in what on many occasions indicated a degree of importance, separate educational systems should have been operated.

From 1948, it will be recalled, when the United Nations sent a mission to Tanganyika to see the trend of developments in this trust territory, the mission urged the government to start integrating the system, as segregation would not lead to harmony of the people, who were working towards one common goal. The British government promised to work towards this unification of the educational system but this was mere lip service. Returning to Tanganyika, in 1954, the mission still urged integration and pointed out that, "the roots of an integrated society cannot go very deep until the individual who belong to it meet on common ground in the formative years of their childhood".

But still the government was not so keen to integrate the system, at least not from below. It suggested doing it from the top, that is at university level, for example at Makerere, at Nairobi Royal Technical College and at Dar-es-Salaam Technical Institute. Unfortunately, so few European and Indian children joined the above educational institutions in East Africa since they were always looking for opportunities to go abroad for courses at university level and then return or stay there. Thus the British Government in answer to the United Nations Mission in 1954 wrote:

> It is further observed that the suggestion that there should be racial unification in primary schools runs counter to the opinion of the majority of educationists who, throughout the world, emphasize the necessity in the case of primary education for schools to be related to social and home environments, and the advisability of teaching the very young in their mother tongue or in the language they use in home environment. There are therefore good grounds for maintaining that government policy in regard to primary education is right and that gradual development towards unification in education from the bottom is less likely to inspire the advance of African education and more likely to be unsuccessful.[4]

Further, the government justified its case claiming that education for Asians and Europeans was not preparing them to live in Tanganyika. Once their fathers were transferred the children would follow, or they would go away on their own volition. However, this was not entirely true. Asians seldom left the territory or, when they left they went to live in Uganda or in Kenya seeking better business opportunities, and life hardly differed there from that of Tanganyika.

But they carried their superiority complex gained over the years, emphasised by this separate education. As for the Europeans perhaps the contention that European children were bound to return to Britain at the end of their parents' career in Tanganyika was to some extent correct. Nevertheless, studying separately continued to give these children a colonial mentality. Once grown up they took up employment in the colonial service and some of them displayed superiority to Africans.

Both Europeans and Asians were quite averse to the idea of integration and the government did not want to force the matter to cause racial animosity from the European and Asian communities. It was also felt that the Asians and Europeans had a right to retain separate education systems because they were the ones paying for the facilities in a greater part. In reply to the United Nations Mission of 1954, the government wrote:

While the objective of the Mission is fully appreciated, the administering authority feels that, so long as the non African communities are making special contributions to the cost of education of the children, and so long as it is impossible, without these extra contributions to the cost of education of their children, to provide from general revenues the educational facilities required by these communities, the communities concerned should have some control over the funds and the institutions to which they specially contribute. When it is possible to dispense with these extra contributions, and yet provide the facilities required, it is agreed that a single unified control would be preferable.[5]

Indeed integration was quite difficult because the people in power were not for it, and it was their children who were going to be integrated. If integration became really necessary it must be carried out in gradual steps. For example a member of the Legislative Council who was in charge of social services, which included education, in the course of his speech made remarks which were revealing. He said:

St. Michael's and St. George's schools at Iringa have been designed and are intended to the education of European children, girls and boys respectively, requiring boarding school education in Tanganyika. At the moment it is recognized that inspite of the rapidly improving and more widespread facilities for secondary education of the children of other races in the Territory, there are children of the other races in the Territory whose parents wish them to have an education of he type they would obtain in an English public school and are prepared and able to pay the fees for such education. It is therefore proposed that when the two separate schools at Iringa, St. Michael's for the girls and St. George's for boys, are fully completed and if surplus accommodation is them available, these schools provided that their normal mode of life is such as to make it possible for them to fit happily into a boarding school of a European type and that their parents are able to pay the fees. The number of non-European children so admitted must necessarily be limited to a small number, the purpose of the schools being to meet the needs of European children for secondary boarding school education.[6]

Very close to the independence date, when it was inevitably realised that the African was going to be his own master, the integration of racially separate institutions became an urgent matter. In December 1958, a committee on racial education was set up and was instructed to consider how the existing three systems could be integrated so as to have a single system of education in Tanganyika. The majority of the members were Europeans and Asians and the whole tone of the Committee's report was for non-integration. Nevertheless, integration was achieved in 1962 and confirmed by an ordinance.

Education for Muslim Children Lagged Behind

As far as school education was concerned, the Muslims had a bad start. In a period when virtually all school education was in the hands of religions denominational groups, all that the Muslim communities had were the Koran schools. The first reason for this was that the Muslims were divided among themselves. The Arabs, especially on the coast and in towns, wanted separate schools for their children whom they did not like to attend African schools. The Arabs maintained that their children had to learn the Arabic language, and that they could not do this in schools that catered for Africans as well. There was also a prevalent philosophy at that time that different races should attend different schools, as White and brown people considered themselves superior to the Black people.

Secondly, Tanganyika Muslims did not have a titular head who could unite them and give them a lead, nor did they have a central organisation to supply trained teachers other than Koran teachers. This constituted a handicap to their educational progress as compared to the Christians. This handicap received mention in the Education Report of 1941, which among other things said:

Nevertheless the fact remains that since the separation of the Territory and in particular the coast from Zanzibar, the Muslim community in Tanganyika has been and still is, handicapped by the lack of a titular head, a central, organization and supply of trained teachers, such as Christian missions can command.[7]

There were several enthusiastic Muslims, however, who set up schools for Muslims. But the absence of a titular head to encourage them and perhaps negotiate on their behalf with the government often made their work difficult and often unsuccessful.

It may be asked why Muslims did not send their children to Christian schools. It will be recalled that, as stated earlier on in this account, the missionaries were given a freehand by government to decide whether or not to admit pupils of another creed into their schools. They exercised this to a considerable degree. Although they were given grants-in-aid, while operating the schools, missionaries at the same type expounded and articulated the Christian philosophy behind education. This activity reasonably alienated Muslims who looked on the exercise as meant to convert all people into Christians. The Muslim parents feared that their children would be converted if they studied in Christian schools. The result of all this was for Muslims to promote their Koran schools, of which there were over 2,000 in 1941 in Tanganyika. The academic quality of these institutions however, was negligible as they mainly gave their pupils knowledge of the Islam faith and not really much in addition.

As time went on the Muslims realised that if their children were to be on equal footing with children from Christian schools, a measure of secular knowledge must be seriously introduced in their Koran schools. The Muslim community also began to complain of government's negligence of the education for their children and of its lack of support of the Muslim system of education (Koran Schools).

Some of the of government's comments on the complaints raised appeared in the department of education report 1941 which read as follows:

> Another interesting and promising sign of the awakening in regard of education is the movement of the Muslim population in favour of a measure of secular education. There is a feeling among a number of Arab and African Muslims that there has been a tendency on the part of government not to pay sufficient attention to the school system which they had built up in pre-European days. This feeling may not be altogether without foundation although it should be noted that in the past many Mohammedan parents have been not a little suspicious of government's educational intentions. Again, in some areas the role of government and Native Administration schools is practically composed of Mohammedan pupils and it has always been government's endeavour to staff these schools with Mohammedan teachers.[8]

With the above in view the government set up a Muslim teacher training centre at Bagamoyo in 1943, to produce Muslim teachers for Muslim schools. This effort of the government had its dividends and Muslim education flourished, so much so that one does not see a great difference between Tanganyika Muslims on one hand and the members of other religions on the other.

Female Education Lagged Behind

Thirdly, as part of the criticism, female education lagged behind male education for too long. British administrators always showed concern over this state of affairs. When, for instance, Chief Kadaha and Chief Sapi, in the Council meeting of 26th November, 1956/1958, urged the Government to speed up the pace of the advance of girl's education, they received full support from the government. In probing the problem of girls' education, the director had found two explanations, which he briefly gave as:

(a) Opposition to girls education in some quarters, because since at primary level it was co-education, it would have been easy for the number of girls to be at par with that of the boys. Did some parents prefer having boys admitted rather than girls?

(b) At post-primary level, lack of locally obtained women teachers necessitating engaging expatriate women teachers who were not only expensive but difficult to get, made the establishment of post primary schools difficult. Consequently, the number of girls is such schools available, were accordingly relatively very small. Statistics extracted from the 1960 Annual Summary of the Ministry of Education Statistics, vividly illuminate the ground for concern.

Primary	4th Year	Middle School	Secondary School
		4th Year	6th Year
Male	59,389	6,724	80
Female	26,244	1,309	4

Again numbers show considerable decline as you move up the school, for instance:

Middle School				Secondary School					
1	2	3	4	1	2	3	4	5	6
2,741	2,143	1,555	1,309	199	188	49	36	4	4

Lack of Facilities for Post-Secondary Education for Africans
Fourthly, no facilities were provided for post-secondary education for Africans within the territory. This is true, but it was possible to send people to Makerere College later on known as the University College of East Africa, which was the only place which offered higher education. Kenya, too, did not have such facilities but there were places for post-school training:

(a) Three teacher training colleges in 1952, could, for instance, absorb students who had completed Standard 10.

(b) There were many departmental training institutions, medical, agriculture, forestry, railways, posts and telegraphs. Many school leavers could go to these for further education. It must be pointed out, however, that the seriousness of absence of facilities for higher education in the Territory, was heavily underlined when government began to consider Africanisation of the civil service. The people who had the required qualifications were not there in the required numbers. But then which country had them? Uganda and Kenya had the same problem.

The Dual System Continued too Long

Lastly, the dual system of education started by the Germans, i.e. government Schools and Voluntary Agencies' schools, was continued too long. It continued the extent that, except in the early part of the period under review, the administration paid grants to voluntary agencies for the salaries of teachers and for equipment and a certain amount of maintenance, and through ordinances controlled what was taught and who was to teach in any school no matter what the owner was. So, the dual system had meaning on paper only.

In practice, government and voluntary agencies' schools were under the department of education. However, there are two complaints arising because of the dual system:

(a) There was no Unified Teaching Service.

(b) The disparity of conditions of service between those who taught in schools operated by voluntary agencies and those who taught in government schools was disheartening. There was such difference in terms of rate of pay and even accommodation.

Schools, Technical and Vocational Training Centres, and Teacher Training Colleges in Tanganyika at Independence

About a month before the day Tanganyika ceased to be a colony the answers to the above questions could be summarised as follows:-

(a) (I - IV)	2,730
Government and otherwise	100
(b) (V - VIII)	
All	480
Unaided	20
(c) (IX - XII)	
Total	42
Unaided	1
Total enrolment	
Primary	450,644
Middle	55,616
Secondary	6,031 of whom 297 were on H.S.C courses.
Technical and Vocational Centres	3,421

Technical, Vocational and Teacher Training Centres

(a) Technical and vocational training centres, 20 all operated by government or local authorities.

(b) Teacher training centres 21 in number
Number of teachers

Primary and Middle	9,190
Secondary	331
Teacher Training	154
Technical and Vocational	62

20

How Agriculture Education failed

As elsewhere in East Africa, in Tanganyika the importance of agricultural education was always stressed. But, perhaps the Central Education Committee of 1939 indicated in clearer language what the aim of the agriculture education programme was. The Committee said:

> We thus advocate a rural educational system consisting of village day schools from which pupils may be selected to enter Rural Middle Schools serving a group of village day schools. From the highest class of the Rural Middle Schools pupils will be selected to enter the provincial teacher training centre or the industrial section attached thereto. The majority, however, will return to their homes and there form what may be described as an educated middle class with an agricultural bias.[9]

It was hoped that the middle class with an agricultural bias would form a nucleus of people who would be open to new ideas in agriculture, influence through example people who had not had a chance of going to school to use improved methods on their *shambas*. Furthermore, according to the committee, agriculture was the pivot of rural education and the answer to those who all the time criticised the education system as too academic.

The committee, therefore, proposed an education system in which agricultural training would figure more prominently than previously. Village schools comprising Primary One to Primary Four would teach simple biology, and school gardening in individual plots to include major district crops. Rural middle schools, Primary Five to Primary Eight, would teach rural science and practical work in agriculture and animal husbandry. The teacher training centres would train teachers to teach these subjects effectively once posted to schools. Some serving teachers would be sent to district agricultural institutions at Ukiriguru and Tengeru to learn methods of teaching agriculture in schools.

In 1947, at the inauguration of the Ten-Year Education Development Plan, Mr. Swynnerton of the Department of Agriculture was asked to make a report on agricultural education and to suggest a new approach to the teaching of the subject in schools. He recommended the introduction of more agriculture courses in schools and agricultural activities where school location allowed it. At first the department of agriculture supervised the teaching of agriculture in schools, but it was later handed over to the department of education.

The agricultural institutions of Tengeru and Ukiriguru continued to brief serving teachers as to how the subject should be taught in schools, and these teachers were distributed all over the country to serve in primary schools. In the 1950's agricultural educational in Middle Schools particularly, received unprecedented stress. Its role in rural reconstruction was much stressed. The Annual Report 1950 of the Education Department said:

> A Middle school in one area should be a school serving a group of villages and closely related to the life of the community and designed to meet its needs. Agriculture and crafts should be taught to produce educated middle class people in villages, the absence of which is felt by many engaged in rural re-construction to be the most serious obstacle to progress.[10]

The elaborate plans for agricultural training of teachers to work in rural schools, plus year to year policy statements from the education department go a long way to show how seriously agriculture was taken in the school programme. The role of a teacher with agricultural training in rural transformation was interestingly described by the Education Department Report of 1950, which said:

> The teacher's life should be a copy for those around him. His own house and shamba should be an example to his neighbours. He should concern himself by means of sports, games, reading circles, the Scout movement and the part he can play in district exhibitions to stimulate a fuller realization of what village life can offer.[11]

In schools such teachers were to be in charge of the school garden, and to instruct the pupils in agricultural skills. Their lessons would start in the classroom and move out to *shambas* for effective practical application. Their pupils would be taught about crop storage methods, new seeds etc., and how to write statistical records; they would be in charge of gardens, crops and records at school. Some of the institutions which had strong agricultural programmes were Mpwapwa and Bwiru Government Teacher Training School where students received thorough training in as much agricultural and animal husbandry work as would be required in the large rural middle schools. Malangali Junior Secondary School was also not able for its agricultural and animal husbandry work which was carried on without any detriment to the academic standards. The Roman Catholic Benedictine Mission School at Peramiko and the Moravian Society School at Usike, near Tabora, were again notable for their effective approach to the practical training of rural school teachers.

Despite the emphasis on the benefits which agricultural education would confer on those who received it, many Tanganyikans thought there was just too much of it particularly in the Middle School. The parents for example, especially protested against too much agricultural education. Their persistent protests caused the United Nations Mission to Tanganyika in 1950 to report and recommend as follows:-

The Mission believes, in view of the great number of protests it received from Africans regarding the amount of time spent, particularly in the Middle Schools on agricultural and practical training, that the administering authority (Britain) might review the matter in order to ensure that the time spent on these subjects does not affect the teaching of the more academic subjects. It might be possible to arrange some of these activities out of school hours or as home projects under the supervision of the agricultural officers 10[10]

The parents it seems, saw the time spent on the subject as merely cutting down valuable time which should be spent on the academic subjects which would entitle a boy or a girl to office employment, and one can easily sympathise with this kind of thought, given the Tanganyika situation where there was a great shortage of trained manpower to work in the government and private sector. The mission's recommendation gave further support to this line of thought.

As already seen in this account agriculture in the middle school became the subject of a fierce debate in 1958 after which it floundered.

Notes
1. Tanganyika Education Department Annual Report 1929, Government Printer Dar-es-Salaam 1929.
2. Ibid.
3. Ibid.
4. United Nation Visiting Mission to Tanganyika 1954, United Nations.
5. Reply to United Nations Mission 1954, Government Printer Dar-es-Salaam, 1954.
6. Proceedings of the Tanganyika Legislative Council, 26 May to 16 June 1959, Government Printer, Dar-es-Salaam 1959.
7. Tanganyika Education Department Annual Report 1941, Government Printer Dar-es-Salaam 1941.
8. Deliberations of the Central Education Committee 1939, Education Department Annual Report 1939, Government Printer Dar-es-Salaam.
9. Tanganyika Education Department Annual Report 1950, Government Printer Dar-es-Salaam.
10. Ibid.

PART FOUR

DEVELOPMENT OF EDUCATION IN ZANZIBAR 1900-1920

21

Education in Zanzibar 1900-1920

Koran Schools

Long before 1900, in Zanzibar, children's spiritual and moral welfare was cared for by the Koran schools which date back to the 7th Century when Muslims from the Persian Gulf began to seek asylum in Zanzibar from their political and religious persecutors. In the Koran schools children learnt to read and to write in Arabic and eventually these two exercises were extended to the Kiswahili language but using the Arabic characters. Religion tended to take the upper hand in the training of boys and girls in the Koran schools. Pupils were required to learn by heart the first 20 chapters of the Koran thereby becoming graduates (Hitimus) of these Koran schools.

The following statement on Koran schools shows what they were like and what their function was:-

> It is necessary to record here that it is considered to be the duty of every good Muslim parent to see that his children hitimu (graduate) that is to say, they learn to read to repeat by heart the Koran. Each village has usually its Koran teachers who gain in livelihood largely through this work, the size of their classes being determined by their ability as teachers and the respect in which they are held by the village people, so that you could find a Koran teacher with 30 pupils due to this difference. This system of religious instruction is an integral part of the village social structure[1].

Unfortunately, when government schools were founded the Koran schools were too ignorant to be used as base or part and parcel of the whole system like in the Christian set-up where catechism classes are held. So, where people felt annoyed at the omission their children deserted government schools and where the people supported government education, they sent their sons attend the local Koran school first or insisted upon dual attendance at both schools. Thus many boys went to the government school in the morning and the Koran teacher in the afternoon.

Other educational influences existed before Western education, if we take a broad view of education as training for life. There existed a whole system of manual training for the work of the fields, fishing and village crafts in which the teaching was by father to son as the two worked together in the struggle against nature. Thus the "agricultural bias", a phrase which has been so common with today's politicians, already existed. Children were brought to realize, as they worked with their parents in the most practical way possible, that their future existence depended upon a life of hard toil in the field as cultivators or on the sea as fishermen. So what was termed rural education from 1920 had existed in Zanzibar before the coming of the Western educational system.

While this kind of education was going on Sultan Seyyid Ali bin Hamoud realized by 1900 that there was an urgent need for a government system of education somewhat based on the British system of education. He felt that the Koran system of education was too religious to allow his Zanzibar's people to participate fully and more usefully in the work of running a state along British lines. He thus in 1903 applied to the Egyptian Government for three teachers to form the nucleus of a staff capable of initiating a scheme of secular education. This would begin in the township and would eventually extend to the more populous districts of the territory.

Egyptian Teacher Sheik Abd el Bari Opens a Primary School in Zanzibar

After an interval of two years, one of the three Egyptian teachers asked for, and called Sheikh Abd el Bari, arrived. He opened a government primary school in Zanzibar town. His difficulties for initiating a new type of educational institution were enormous mostly because the Muslims of Zanzibar did not at once have confidence in the new institution. The Christian missionaries had introduced schools on both Zanzibar and Pemba islands to cater for the freed slaves who had been brought from far afield in the hinterland of East Africa. Their schools also sought economic opportunities in the islands. The attendance at these European oriented schools had led to the eventual christianising of both the freed slaves, their children and the free people on the main land who had come to seek economic opportunities. So, starting a primary school different from a Koran school, though headed by a fellow Muslim could not fail to arouse suspicion on the islands. Therefore, at first there was less enthusiastic welcome to Abd el Bari's school.

The First Director of Education Rivers Smith and Problems of Organising Zanzibar's Education System 1907-1910

Feeling that the exercise was too much for him alone, Sheikh Abd el Bari suggested that the government appoints a European to undertake the task of establishing an education system on British lines. In 1907, in response to an application to the Foreign Office, Rivers-Smith was seconded from the Egyptian education service to Zanzibar for three years as director of education.

The problem with which Rivers-Smith was faced may best be understood if we give here a brief review of the social and economic conditions obtaining in the then Protectorate of Zanzibar at the beginning of the 20th Century. It was inevitable, when Sultan Seyyid Said transferred his capital from Muscat at Zanzibar in 1844, that the life of the Arab land owning aristocracy gradually became more closely integrated with the slave population on which the domestic and economic life of the protectorate so largely depended. In the course of time, partly as a result of concubinage and inter-marriage, Kiswahili became more and more the language of the Arab homes. Whereas the Koran schools back in Muscat may have provided facilities for very elementary secular education through the medium of Arabic, the Arabs in Zanzibar at the turn of the century could not offer even this rudimentary service.

With the abolition of slavery in Zanzibar in 1897, the plantation owners were faced with a new set of circumstances to cope with which the standard of education of the adult generation proved to be inadequate, while that of the younger generation was limited to *hitimu* or the ability to repeat the first 20 chapters *(suras)* of the Koran by heart. The educational value of this achievement will be appreciated when it is stated that at the time Seyyid Ali made the first move the children of an increasing number of Arab families spoke little or no Arabic at all in the home.

As a result of the changed conditions many land owners found themselves in financial difficulties, with their properties heavily mortgaged. At the same time practically all skilled trade had become an Asian monopoly. The success of the plan for education rested in the hope of the rehabilitation of the once prosperous plantation owners and the establishment of the sultan's subjects firmly in the skilled labour market. The only possible medium in the elementary stages was Kiswahili, but because the protectorate was Mohammedan it was essential to recognize the need for the study of the Koran and inclusion of Arabic as a subject of study in the curriculum. There seemed little doubt that the old Arab families visualised in education a channel through which the prestige of their language might be restored.

The written medium of communication was at this time largely Kiswahili in Arabic characters. To have recruited teachers with a knowledge of Latin alphabet, indicating a Christian mission education, would only have added to the existing suspicion. The confidence of the parents was the first prerequisite to progress and it was therefore decided to explore the possibility of collecting a group of the better village Koran teachers and give them an elementary course of teacher training with a view of introducing simple instruction in the 3 Rs, through the medium of Kiswahili in Latin characters on their return, to their village schools.

But it was decided to introduce English in the curriculum at the government primary school in 1907 to counter-balance the Arab suspicion to teaching their Kiswahili, a language the Arabs treated as one for the slaves although they were using it in their homes. At the same time Abd el Bari was asked to assist the director of education to start a teacher training school. Indeed, with the very poor material available a high standard of efficiency could not at first be expected. But the definite step forward was made which justified the building of an improved type of village school in one or two more populous areas.

In the early stages enrolment was poor and attendance piece-meal. Some officials even considered the question of compulsory attendance since education was offered free of charge to attract parents and pupils. But it was eventually considered too premature a step which could even bring about resistance from the Arab population. Suspicion too of the intentions of the government for this kind of education was still an obstacle. It could only disappear when there was concrete evidence of the material benefits to be derived from the new system. Some village schools were closed due to lack of support prior to 1914.

Since the economy of the protectorate was primarily agricultural it seemed clear that the immediate objective should be to give the educational system an agricultural bias at the top. The education development plan of 1907 visualized a post-primary boarding school in a rural area, more particularly for the sons of Arab plantations owners with a view to equipping them for the better management of their estates. It was also hoped that a school in such an environment would have provided a good setting for the training of teachers.

Post-primary courses and teacher training were still in the realm of the future. By 1909 the primary school could claim to be well organised with a three-year elementary course followed by four years in English, leading to the Primary Leaving Certificate Examination, for which the Arabic language was a compulsory subject. The reason for the adoption of a local standard, rather than affiliation to a public examination body in England, was the danger of a wrong sense of the value of an English certificate in the early stages of a system of education in the African countries. It was however to the credit of the teaching staff, that the examination at once achieved its object as a qualification for the junior clerical service of the government and a satisfactory standard from which to proceed to secondary education when this became possible. This fact was emphasised by the readiness of the Egyptian government to accept the Zanzibar Certificate as a qualification for entrance to one of their secondary schools. And one of the first group of pupils who passed out of the primary school went on to Cairo for secondary education.

Beginnings of Technical Education

While the primary school course was being organised, the equally important subject of industrial apprenticeship was appreciated. But at that time the age of pupils had little relation to normal classroom standards and the beginning could only be on modest lines. It was eventually decided that the qualification should be the completion of the three years. Both admittedly inadequate but the best that could be hoped for to make a beginning.

Though the plan had been decided upon, its implementation still seemed to present almost insurmountable difficulties. Where for instance, could an instructor be found? The field of selection was limited to Asian artisans. Would an instructor of sufficient skill have the courage to risk the hostility of his community by accepting responsibility for the training of Zanzibar subjects to take their place in the skilled labour market and so threaten the monopoly hitherto enjoyed? In Damji Purshotam, however, the department of education found a highly skilled craftsman and a very loyal servant in spite of the intrigue by other craftsmen of his Asian community.

The appointment of a craftsman to take charge of instruction was however only the first of the many difficulties which has to be overcome. Though highly skilled, Damji was not a trained instructor. He had no idea of working to a syllabus. He had to teach drawing to get his trade arithmetic over, he had to learn a new calligraphy and had to teach in a foreign language. But such was his enthusiasm that he overcame all the difficulties, and a most promising course for joinery apprentices was soon up and running smoothly. A course in tailoring was started shortly afterwards and proved of no little value in the years that followed.

Plans to establish the young artisans in the skilled labour market had however, to be made well in advance as previous attempts made my missions had failed. One reason had been that no provision has been made to ensure that, on the completion of his training, the apprentice possessed the tools of his trade, so that given the initiative, he could set up a business for himself. This difficulty had been provided for under the new scheme of apprenticeship. A small monthly allowance was made to apprentices, but half of this allowance was held against the completion of the three years' course and then paid to the young artisan in the form of a set of tools of his trade. But a still greater difficulty had to be met.

It was generally understood that hitherto the young Zanzibari aspiring to skilled industry, had been quietly squeezed out by his more experienced Indian competitor, who employed him merely as his mate to carry the bag of tools. This manipulation achieved its object and the closed shop persisted to try and overcome this difficulty. An ex-apprentices' workshop plan was made, it was recognized, as mentioned, that a period of three years was inadequate to train a full craftsman, and experience had shown that there was little chance of his standing on his own.

He needed sympathetic supervision and guidance for a longer period to improve his skill and to gain experience until such time as a sufficiently strong group could be launched in the labour market as a body. An educational dream of these early days was that a co-operative public works department would, in some undefined future, provide the systematic foreman and the job on which young Zanzibar artisans could demonstrate their worth.

The organisation of the shop pre-supposed the provision of machinery for the rough work so that more attention could be given to the advanced skills of the craft. Jobs had to be forthcoming to keep the numbers fully occupied. Price rates had to be fixed on a scale to make the output competitive while ensuring a fair living wage and living scope of enterprise which would bring a corresponding reward. All these aspects of the problem had to be carefully weighed and Damji threw himself heart and soul into the new adventure. It was realized that in order for the plan to be successful it must largely depend in the first instance on permission being obtained to make furniture for the government.

With the fairly good wood-working machinery and motors the new shop ran on well from the beginning but unhappily, the experience was denied the opportunity of providing its value. After only two years of its existence war broke out and the department of education was one of the institutions earliest to experience a shortage of funds.

For example, after naval disaster of 20th September 1914, the survivors from the *HMS Pergasus* established a base ashore, taking over the workshops of the railway and electricity department.

The apprentices' shop, the only one in the Protectorate, was taken over and the young artisans were dispersed and were absorbed into war activities. From 1914 until 1920 the department of education and the whole educational system were almost entirely deprived of leadership and they could hardly claim to have done more than mark time.

22

Searching for an Education Policy 1920 - 1940

Emphasis on Rural Education?

After the First World War as already mentioned elsewhere, the British colonial policy came out openly in support of a sound education system in the colonies. The Zanzibar government set up a committee in 1920 to determine the type of educational policy to be followed.

The aim was largely to promote better methods of agriculture. It was planned that in future education should help those who could avail themselves of it to be better at managing their rural life and have less need to forsake village life for town life. In short, rural education was emphasised. A large majority of the pupils of the rural schools were Africans and the schools were mostly for them but the Arab culture made a dominant influence among the Africans in all parts of the territory.

From the practical point of view, results of rural education were not impressive and many parents stated that they considered these practical subjects a waste of time. They argued, with some justification, that if it was agriculture that the boys were to be taught, then the parents were competent to teach them in their own fields with some practical benefits accruing there from. Similarly the village carpenter was said to be capable of giving better instruction than that given in schools.

Rural Education Policy Becomes Difficult to Implement

The rural education policy was difficult to implement. Firstly, the parents had hoped that their sons were going to schools primarily to qualify and get paid employment in government departments and the private sector. Secondly, the teacher training school opened in 1923 at Zanzibar town did not train teachers in such a way that they would stress the rural side of the education. No course for teaching agriculture was ever given to them. How could they then teach agriculture? Moreover, most of the students who joined the teacher training college were town-bred. These hated the idea of going to teach in the villages where the situation was so different from that of the town. They thus went to countryside schools unhappily and while teaching they hardly stressed the agricultural and technical side of school work. They gave a predominantly academic primary course to the pupils. Pupils had the impression that they were attending schools not to go back to the land but to get employment in town. Yet when they returned home they showed a very big disinclination to work on the family farms. The attitude of their sons made parents all the more disillusioned about school education.

Government Attack on Koran Schools Causes Desertion of Government Primary Schools

Meanwhile the government opened a war on the Koran system of schools. It thought that these schools, which taught children mainly by heart to recite the first 20 chapters of the Koran and Muslim prayer had no sound approach to education. But in a Muslim community, such schools and their methods of teaching are part and parcel of the Muslim religious heritage. This attack was, however, unjustified because if one examined the conditions and the methods in Christian catechumen schools, they hardly differed from those of the Koran schools. The conditions of the catechumen schools were squalid and the methods of teaching were those whereby children learnt by heart things they hardly comprehended although they were in the vernaculars.

Thus the education fostered in Zanzibar by the government was seen as meant to render the Muslim children economically useless because these children would not get paid employment on leaving primary schools and when back to the land they did not like to work. Also, the education was viewed as intended to render their children religiously unfit as the traditional Koran schools were being discredited. The government, however provided Koran lessons in the primary syllabus. Here the snag was that pupils learnt the Koran much slower than in proper Koran schools because in the primary schools the pupils had to be taught the Arabic language first so that they could understand what they were learning in the Holy book.

This was quite a slower process and parents were not slow in making comparisons with those children who had refused to join the primary schools but remained at the Koran schools or those who attended primary schools in the morning and attended the Koran schools in the afternoon. They found out that the pupils at government primary schools were backward in the knowledge of the Holy Book and parents were able to point out that the government primary schools were not adequate for the function of teaching religion, which was considered to be the major duty of any school in a Muslim community. Moreover, the war on Koran schools meant that all such schools were not wanted. Yet there were parents who did not want to send their children to the government primary schools. Where would then such children learn the vital knowledge of the Koran? As a result the Koran teachers put up a very determined fight to make the government primary schools fail. This was possible since they had a greater influence on the people than the European government officials who did not come into people's homes and join in their prayers and parties especially of a religion nature.

The result of all this was that from about 1935 primary schools which had been opened all during the 1920s by government were being deserted gradually so much so that teachers had no work and they were being seconded as clerks to government departments. Eventually the teacher training college was closed down in 1935. This gradual breaking down of the educational system in Zanzibar was the subject of the commission of inquiry of 1939. The commission revealed that the education system was bound to collapse completely because the policy then followed did not take into account the people's feelings and aspirations and the education given to teachers was not preparing them to fulfil the aims of the policy. So from 1940 the government set out to try and regain the confidence of the Muslim population.

Government Acceptance of Koran Schools and Free Primary Education

The government accepted the fact that Koran schools could not be destroyed by discouraging them. What was needed was to accept them in the educational system as they also engaged in useful educational work. This step removed a major source of friction between the schools and the people. The government set up a system of giving some grants-in-aid to some of the Koran schools so that they could better the conditions under which they were running. For example, they would put up better buildings in which they ran their lessons instead of being run on the house verandahs of Koran teachers.

The government also attached a Koran class to each government primary school as the first class and it employed Koran teachers who were supported and had been selected by the community in which the school was situated. This step helped to increase the Muslims' support for government primary schools. The Koran teachers usually brought their pupils with them to join the Koran class attached to each primary school which decreased the number of independent Koran schools. As Koran classes in government primary schools devoted nearly all the time to religious teaching, this helped to reduce the number of religion lessons in the normal primary schools. In 1940 there were 871 Koran schools with 6,223 pupils. Some of these schools were called "schools" only by courtesy because many of them only contained one or two pupils being taught on a verandah of a *mwalimu* teacher.

Enthusiasm for education was also aroused by giving primary education free of charge to those children who came forward to be taught. So anybody who wanted to send his child to school could do so without fearing meeting the financial charges. A policy was also initiated especially train Arabs for positions of leadership within the government. The colonisers had tended to take up all positions of power and the Arabs saw no chance of getting them even if they had availed themselves of education. This had also discouraged them from sending their children to school during the inter-war period.

23

Zanzibar's Structure of Education and its Development Under the British Administration 1930-1963

(a) Infant Schools

At the beginning of the system there were infant schools run privately and they took in just a few children of those parents who wished for this kind of education and could. The number of these infant schools was quite negligible for by 1960 there were only four of them and yet that was when the demand for education had grown so high that the government could not cope with it with the existing financial situation of the protectorate. Also, to each girls primary school was attached an infant class for purposes of teaching girls childcare. So where in the boys primary schools a Koran class had been attached, in the girl's school it was an infant class. No fees were charged.

(b) Primary Schools

The majority of these primary schools belonged to the government. In fact the government by 1960 had 50 boys' primary schools and 13 girls' primary schools. The Asian community had 7 grant-aided primary schools some of which were attached to secondary schools and the Christian missions had four primary schools. Besides these, there were private primary schools. Koran classes could be attended for a year or more and then the pupils who had completed the necessary Koran studies would either return home or go to join the primary classes proper. Pupils could proceed from the private Koran schools to join government primary schools. This indeed reassured the Muslim community that these Koran schools were part of the education system of the protectorate.

A full primary course was eight years, but there were very few schools of this grade. The majority ran from Primary One to Primary Six and then sent their pupils to the few schools which had a full primary course. Thus Primary Six was also considered to be a break in the primary course and pupils sat for an examination to proceed to Primary Seven and Eight. Many pupils indeed ended their education at primary six stage.

What Was Taught in Primary Schools?

Besides the academic subjects there was an attempt to make the course a bit practical by teaching agriculture theoretically and practically the school garden with a common sight at each school. The department of agriculture helped in advising the teachers as to how to teach agriculture. Food for school meals and for home consumption was grown on these gardens and fortunately in the countryside they had an influence on the people's agricultural habits. People used to look at the gardens as models to be followed on their farms and they indeed followed them. Thus in a way these primary schools were acting as an instrument of change within the communities in which they were situated. On the technical side, the schools taught handicraft where mat-weaving, tool-making and many other simple village crafts were practised.

But agriculture and art crafts never dominated the school curriculum and although most of the pupils after primary school education returned to the land it was not so much because of a change of attitude brought about by education; it was rather that jobs for all could not be found in town. Yet parents never resented this so much as they did in the 1930s. One explanation of this is that the policy pursued during the inter-war period was to carry on education divorced from the wishes of the people of the protectorate. But once these people saw that they had a part to play in the system, they supported the venture even if it meant their children going back to the land after taking the bother of attending these schools. They had also realised that to cope up in a world where Western influence had come to replace the Arabic influence their children had to get this kind of education as a means of survival.

What was the Medium of Instruction?

Kiswahili was the medium of instruction in these primary schools and English was only taught as a subject from Primary Four, while Arabic was taught right from the Koran classes. There was one primary school in Zanzibar town called the Muslim School. This used Arabic in teaching children. There was a wish from the Arabs to set up primary schools that would use Arabic alone as a medium of instruction, but this was seen as unrealistic by the government because only a few children from some Arab homes could speak the language. Nearly all Arab homes spoke Kiswahili as a result of a long custom that grew up even before the beginning of the 16th Century, which gradually rendered Arabic to be a dead language in Zanzibar. This had been brought about mostly by two phenomena, one the inter-marriages between Arab men and African women, although African young men hardly married Arab girls because of the Arab customs of girls not mixing freely with young men. It was quite difficult for African young men to meet the young Arab women whereas on the side of Arab men generally African families used to come from the rural areas and settle on Arab clove plantations as workers. As these produced daughters the daughters would be adopted by Arab landlords. These daughters would grow in the Arab homes adopting Islam and Arab customs, Arab young men could easily pick them up as wives. These African girls spoke Kiswahili.

The demand for using Arabic as a medium of instruction was partly revived in 1958 when a Muslim academy was set up with Arabic as part of the curriculum at secondary school level. But by 1960 the government was advising it to include other subjects lest pupils attending it did not compete on equal terms with those who were attending other schools. The academy, however, never had an effect on society as a Muslim Institution.

The Problem of Wastage

There used to be wastage at primary school level among both girls and boys. Among girls it was usually the feeling of parents that at a certain age especially as soon as they reached puberty, that they should be removed to get married. This tendency was mostly seen among rural girls and less among urban girls. The education department which had done a lot to persuade parents to send their daughters to school had to devise means of giving them as much educational content as possible before the parents would remove them suddenly.

So their programme at primary level used to be crammed so that before they were suddenly removed they would have had the best possible training for life. This removal of girls before the end of the primary school section made it difficult to get women teachers who were very much needed to help the development of girls schools. During the period under review, all governments in East Africa made a determined attempt to make girls attend school. It was realized that unless women were also educated, men's education would be less effective especially in homes. In the case of women in Zanzibar this was all the more obvious because women's influence had neutralised the Arabic language in homes.

As for boys, especially in rural areas, there was a tendency of removing them by their parents as soon as they reached a certain age at which they could be useful on the family farm. For example, clove picking used to interfere very much with boys' school attendance. This was rather a failure on the part of administration to make school holidays coincide with the clove harvesting.

Although government primary schools mixed African and Arab pupils together, schools in Zanzibar were primarily run on racial lines. Africans and Arabs were lumped together and Asian children attended their own primary schools. It was at secondary level that these races came together. All Asians schools were not directly under the management of the government. They only got grants-in-aid from the government. Asian children had universal primary education and many of them attended secondary schools. European children had no schools except that St. Monica's Convent of the Universities Mission of

Central Africa took on a few European children in the lower primary classes. European education was primarily obtained in Kenya where the children of the European government officers obtained bursaries and transport fare from the Zanzibar government.

The Difficult Road to Secondary Education for Africans

The secondary school section ran from Standard Nine to Standard 12. It was only from 1959 that two classes were added on for the Higher School Certificate course which had hitherto been run at Makerere University College. Education at secondary level, unlike at the primary level, was paid for although there was complete remission or part of fees where parents proved to be quite unable to meet the charges. As a result of this secondary education being paid for, and since most of the Africans lived in rural areas and had to pay for accommodation in hostels in town where the two secondary schools were, fewer of them consequently availed themselves of secondary education and Arabs and Asians took the majority of places at secondary level. Consequently the jobs that were opening up in government and needed secondary and higher education went to the Arabs and to the Asians. Although they policy pursued during this period was to give responsible posts to the people of Zanzibar, this did not affect the Africans in the main. An examination of people appointed as officers in the government shows that it was almost only the Arabs who got these posts of responsibility.

A Commission of Inquiry into Zanzibar's Education in 1958

By 1958 there were so many children graduating at primary school level and the demand for secondary school places became very acute. There were widespread complaints that children had nowhere to go for secondary school education. For example, while over 1,000 pupils sat for Primary Eight examinations every year, there was accommodation for only over 200 pupils in secondary schools by 1958. As a result of this crisis the government appointed a commission of inquiry in the same year to look into the development of education and recommend the future developments of both the secondary and the primary education.

In fact the period under review experienced a terrific change from the inter-war period which had been characterised by people's apathy and distrust of the educational system. So, the development of education during this period was hindered by a shortage of funds rather than by lack of people's demand for it. The following figures can give us an insight into the development. By 1960 there were 50 boys primary schools whereas in 1939 nearly all primary schools had been closed down due to lack of support by the community. There were 12,528 boys in primary school and 944 boys in secondary classes.

Besides these there were 13 girl's primary schools with 7,335 in the primary school and 416 in the secondary school section. According to the 1948 census there were 247,687 Arabs and Africans and 15,246 Asians. So these figures of children attending schools were in proportion to the country's population. All this education was costing the government 14.4 per cent of the protectorate's budget by 1960. The recommendations of the commission for expansion were not however implemented for lack of funds.

Girl's Education Grew Painfully Slowly

But although there was a dramatic growth in the number of children joining schools by 1960, the number of girls grew very slowly at the beginning. Parents had to be persuaded very much to be convinced that girls needed education. And once some of the girls came home their parents could not see the relevance of teaching their daughters for example their language, Kiswahili, after all they knew it. Also the Arab parents were prejudiced against their daughters being taught domestic science because they still felt that child-care and cooking were chores for African servants which chores not long ago were being performed for them by slaves.

So they looked at the exercise as meant to demean their daughters. Moreover, the parents did not envisage their daughters going to work in offices. They thought that the education which their daughters were getting in homes was adequate to make them good wives and mothers. If Arab girls were few in schools African girls were fewer still. Games for girls were also disapproved of by parents although indeed they were necessary because the Arab girls used to spend a very sedentary life sitting all day at the back of their parents' homes. At school these games had to be played within enclosed courtyards on account of observing "purdah".

Gradually, however, girls became interested in education or their parents did. And to excite this interest their teachers usually would take them around the country to give demonstration lessons to village women in home management and in preparing appetising dishes. More parents' interest got aroused that way and they started to feel that their daughters too should be like the girls who were demonstrating to them the modern methods of doing things. By 1943 some girls had started to join secondary classes and in 1947 a secondary school was set up for girls as a result of their number having grown and showing signs of growing even more. The number of girls in primary schools indicated above and that in secondary classes by 1960 does not compare too badly with that of the boys.

We should also mention that although all Koran schools were co-educational, it was not so acceptable for primary schools to be universally co-educational due to Muslim customs where women are supposed to play different roles in society, different from those of men. So only a few primary schools (and at a lower level) practised co-education but by the large girls attended their own schools.

Other channels of education were provided in teachers' colleges, in some technical organisations, at Makerere in Uganda, at the Railway School in Nairobi, in Tanganyika especially at Government school Tanga, in Britain and India.

Teacher Education

By 1960 there were two teacher training colleges: One for men called the Seyyid Khalifa College and the other one for women called the Seyyid Nunu College. These two colleges had been set up as a result of the 1946 Ten-Year Development Plan for Education. It recommended permanent teachers' colleges. Hitherto since the closure of the Zanzibar Teacher Training College in 1935 teachers had been educated at Dole Primary school. In order to avoid repeating the mistake of the inter-war period, the teachers' course consisted of agriculture and handicraft lessons so that they could teach these subjects to the children once they had graduated.

At first those two colleges required students who had finished their Primary Eight course. But from 1952, in a bid to raise standards students were recruited from groups of students who had completed their Standard 12 education and preferably students who had a Cambridge School Certificate. Those recruited at Standard Eight took four years at the course, part of which was to give them more academic content and the other part was spent on the professional side. But those recruited after Standard 12 took only two years which were spent on professional course. All these were meant to teach in the primary schools after graduation. At the secondary school level there were expatriates and graduates from Makerere.

Technical Education

There was no technical school in Zanzibar and it was claimed that if one was set up it was doubtful if the economy of the protectorate would be able to absorb the graduates after a few years. So technical training was limited to the training of apprentice-carpenters and mechanics by the government's works department. Also, some students after Primary Eight were being sent to the industrial classes of some Tanganyika schools especially Tanga Government School.

In 1948 the Mombasa Institute of Muslim Education was opened. The Zanzibar government was financially committed to provide a large part of the running costs and even provided money to set up the institute. The institute was intended to serve the whole of East African Muslim technical educational needs. It gave trade courses up to the intermediate standard of the City and Guilds of London Institute and other corresponding examinations. Between 20 and 25 students wee sent to it from Zanzibar each year for the first four years. After that period it was decided to send just a few students each year for they could not be absorbed on graduation. Finally, in 1958 the Zanzibar government stopped sending students to the institute because it was being required to meet higher and higher running costs of maintaining it. Yet the economy could not absorb graduates of higher qualifications as the government claimed. We must however realise during the colonial days it was necessary to train people to act as assistants to the Europeans. So, while there were many Europeans holding jobs of responsibility of a technical nature the government felt that there was no need to train Arabs and Africans who would replace the Europeans.

There were, however, some sundry technical courses conducted however, on Zanzibar. There was the rural middle school founded in 1935 which was a primary school running from primary five to primary eight. It gave some classes in masonry and carpentry. But its main purpose was to get pupils from other primary schools which had no Primary classes Eight and prepare them adequately for secondary schools. Later in 1956 this school was converted into a purely secondary technical school for boys with courses leading to the Cambridge School Certificate Examinations. The only technical school Kariimjee Trade School, was set up in Zanzibar 1956. Education was not quite relevant. Boys were taught to build stone houses yet nobody could ask to have such houses built for him.

Higher Education

As for post secondary-education there was no institute for students in Zanzibar to cater for it. Students had to go to Makerere in Uganda where some of them did various courses. But up to 1960 the number of Zanzibar students at Makerere never exceeded 12 in one single year. Also, there were scholarships provided by Zanzibar government, by the Colonial Development and Welfare Fund, and by the British Council and these were given to students who went to study in universities in Britain, Arab countries and India.

Administration of the System

In Zanzibar, unlike in the rest of East Africa, the government from 1907 took a leading part in providing education to the people on Western lines. The responsibility for administration was shouldered by the director of education. Zanzibar being a strong hold of Islam could not accept Christian missionaries setting up schools for Muslim children for fear of tampering with their faith. So, the responsibility of setting up the majority of schools and of administering them rested on the government and the government was freer to lay down its educational policy and pursue it while in the rest of East Africa such a policy, if laid down, had to be watered down by the feelings of the missionaries who also wanted education to take a certain inclination.

It was the private Koran schools which did not come under the administration of the government, both those which got grants-in-aid and those which did not. But they were accepted as part and parcel of the education system and each year a few of them were being added to the grants-in-aid list and some of their teachers would be called up to each in the Koran classes attached to government primary schools. Once such teachers were called they would close their Koran schools and proceed with their pupils to the Koran class to which they had been called to serve.

Again outside the direct government administration were schools established by different Asian communities. By 1960 there were seven in number and they got aid from government. Besides these, there were four Christian schools one of which was at Wete but did not get government grants-in-aid. The Holy Ghost Fathers maintained St. Joseph's Convent primary school primarily for Goan children and a few European children where they used English as a medium of instruction. It had a wing for African children also. The Universities Mission to Central African (UMCA) had a school at Kiungani out of Zanzibar and ran two sections one for boys and another for girls. St. Monica Convent catered for mixed races which had no particular school such as some European children and some Goans.

The primary school at Kiungani terminated at Primary Eight and the UMCA sent its students who wanted secondary school education to their school at Minaki near Dar-es-Salaam. The Friends' Industrial Mission had a school on Pemba at Banani. These Christian schools catered for African pupils whose parents were of ex-slave parentage and also for those children whose parents were from the mainland. The Christian missions had made very few converts in Zanzibar among the predominantly Muslim community. The mission schools were traditionally kept to cater for those Africans whom they had come to look after in the second half of the 19th Century.

Besides the above set of schools, there were four private schools which did not get grants-in-aid from the government. These were the Comorian school run by the French government for Comorian pupils who went to Zanzibar from these islands in the Indian Ocean which where under France. Then there was Ithneshery School and Mr. Pota's School, all in the Zanzibar town and the H.H. Aga Khan School.

Decrees and Regulations Made to Enable Government to Develop Education in Zanzibar (1921 - 1963)

In the course of over 40 years, the Government made a number of decrees and regulations as became necessary in order to develop and direct Zanzibar's education system. The most important were as follows:-

1. The Compulsory Education Decree of 1921
    This empowered the British Resident to cause Arab and African children between the ages of five and nine to be enrolled in government schools for stated periods. If a child was not enrolled or played truant, the director of education had power, to ask the police to get him to school.

    The decree was, however, applied rather leniently and since there was no provision for punishing parents for either refusing to enrol their children or for preventing them from non-attendance, the decree was ineffective. That was why parents were free to pull their children out of school during the inter-war period. The decree was amended in 1958 making the parents punishable. But then the provision was no longer as useful as during the period mentioned above. By 1958 most parents were keen on seeing their children in schools and it was only the shortage of schools which frustrated their wish.

2. The Apprentice Decree of 1926
    It provided for the control of apprentices indentured so that there was means of bringing them back if they absconded.

3. The Public Health Decree of 1929
    This empowered the director of education to close down such schools as were unclean, over crowded, badly lighted or ventilated, or insufficiently provided with sanitary arrangements.

4. The Penal Code prevented the use of seditious books or seditious teaching.

5. The Savings Bank Decree, outlined how and when and by whom public money of the school should be banked.

6. The Schools Provident Fund Decree made it obligatory for teachers in grant-in-aided schools to contribute part of their earnings monthly against the day of retirement.

7. Then there were 8 regulations passed between 1961 and 1963 regarding nomenclature and division of schools plus classes, punishments, safety in schools, conditions of admission to government schools, grants-in-aid, school fees to be paid, conduct of schools, award of bursaries and scholarships, contract of training teachers and registration of schools.

By means of these decrees and regulations the educational system was under the close supervision of the government.

Conclusion

The tremendous development of education in Zanzibar Protectorate between 1939 and 1960 was due to the realisation by the government that education had to be identified with the ideas of the Muslim society and that the people had to see themselves as ones accepted to play a leading part in its direction. This was mostly at the lower level with the running of the Koran schools and Koran classes in the government primary school.

PART FIVE

DEVELOPMENT OF EDUCATION SINCE INDEPENDENCE

Introduction

Unhappiness has been expressed over the school system in East Africa. It has been seriously suggested that long after independence the system has continued to be foreign wrenched from a European environment and erected in a society to which it is not related. The programmes it offers are bookish and are geared to preparing pupils for higher education which (whichever way you look at it) still remains the prize goal of small number of pupils.

It has continued to display glaring failure at training pupils for life in national communities. The multiplicity of examinations stifles initiative and innovation in education. Its products continue to look for white collar jobs and display contempt for manual work.

We have earlier in this book indicated that before independence the men responsible for education were often criticised by contemporaries about the education they were offering to East Africans. Even the very people administering and formulating policy for Africans education, tackled the problem of ridding the system of deficiencies. If they were unable to wipe out deficiencies in the system it was not because of incapacity or lack of interest but, rather that the task of providing education for a nation that fits it in an ever changing world is attended by many intractable problems.

Two questions which troubled colonial educationists have continued to trouble independent East Africans. Firstly, how should the activities of the schools be organised so that the school leaver does not shun returning to his locality but should return there to apply his training confidently? Secondly, what do you do to give education to the adult community so that it is not left behind by ever rising numbers of children to whom education is easily available? The search for answers to these questions has in a number of times landed us in the hands of experimenters from overseas who have tried experiments for two years or a year and left with no trace of results of the experiments left behind for us to use. We have held conferences and deliberated over suggested new directions in teacher education, secondary education and adult education. We have for long hours sat to consider innovations in curriculum and teaching that would help us answer the questions but to what extent have we succeeded?

On the credit side, very soon after independence each of the ministries of education in East Africa concentrated its energies on remedying the most visible defects of the system. For instance, each sovereign state expanded facilities for secondary school education, teacher education, and higher education and the results of the exercise are astounding. But making what is taught at school relevant to the needs of East Africans, while it is true it is being tackled, there is still a long way to go. Let it be pointed out that the task is complicated by the fact that East African society is now a part of the large world community. So what is taught at school should be of use locally but when dealing with the rest of the world it should equally be useful. Children at school, and parents at home who have been to school or not, know very well that whether we like it or not, East Africans live in a sophisticated world propelled by science and technology along paths which we have compulsorily to tread (there being no alternative paths).

Whatever the school operators decide to teach must be relevant not only to the East African environment but should be capable of making pupils move with the modern world and, other things being equal, at a pace set by the modern world. There is no choice. Curricula that makes the East African society continue to lag distantly behind the rest of the world in the next century (as has been the case in the current century) have no place and should be discarded. The element of relevancy, must be determined with reference not only to local needs but also to the needs of pupils as members of the world community. A pupil who sees electric wires go to his village and produce light, aeroplanes fly over his village, a radio set bringing to his home a voice from 4,000 miles away, will soon or later protest if what he is taught omits teaching how these products of technology are made and work and indeed how he can make and cause them to work.

With these remarks in mind we would like now to review briefly the main developments and achievements, and highlight challenges encountered in education, which is no longer the business of foreigners but the business and responsibility of the Wanainchi (East Africans), Black East Africans, to be specific. It is not easy to avoid considering each Sate separately if we are to avoid entanglement in generalisations applicable to one or two states and not the rest of the East African Community. Once again let us take Kenya first.

24

Kenya

Embarking on Wide Changes Needed in the Education System

At independence, Kenyan leaders were entrusted with a mission: *KUJENGA NCHI* - to build the nation.

This mission at once would call for wide changes in an education system which a European settler-dominated government had set up with maximum provision for the minority European and Asian groups, and minimum provision for the majority African Kenyans. The following table indicating the number of primary and secondary school pupils (1963) and its relation to school-age population (1962) of the ethnic group to which pupils at school belonged, amply illustrates the point just made.

Primary School

Ethnic Group	No. of Pupils	School-Age Population	% of Pupils of school-age
African	840,677	2,421,300	34.7
Arab	3,222	9,000	36.9
Asian	40,915	52,800	77.5
European	6,639	8,900	74.6

Secondary School

Ethnic Group	No. of Pupils	School-Age population	% of pupils of school-age
African	10,593	829,700	1.3
Arab	292	3,100	9.4
Asian	13,912	17,200	80.9
European	3,265	3,300	98.9

Source: Kenya Ministry of Education Triennial Survey 1961 - 63. Govt. Printer Nairobi. Statistical Abstract 1965, Nairobi p. 6 and 11

The Ominde Education Commission 1963

To give the needed changes a firm foundation and clear direction, in December 1963 the government set up the Kenya Education Commission under the chairmanship of Professor S. H. Ominde whose terms of reference were: to survey the existing educational resources of Kenya and to advise the government in the formation and implementation of national policies for education which:

(a) appropriately express the aspirations and cultural values of an independent African country.

(b) take account of the need for trained manpower for economic development and for other activities in the life of the nation.

(c) take advantage of the initiative and service of regional and local authorities and voluntary bodies.

(d) contribute to the unity of Kenya.

(e) respect the educational needs and capabilities of children.

(f) have due regard for the resources, both in money and in personnel, that are likely to become available for educational services.

(g) provide for the principal educational requirements of adults.

After a thorough-going study of the educational system, the commission put before the government a report which was most illuminating, comprehensive and down-to-earth guiding educational planning document in the history of Kenya's education. The commission made 160 recommendations. One of the most important parts of the report was the clear statement on the purpose of education in independent Kenya. The commission spelt out that purpose as follows:

1. Education is a function of the Kenya nation; it must foster a sense of nationhood and promote national unity.

2. Education in Kenya must serve the people of Kenya and the needs of Kenya without discrimination.

3. Our public schools are an instrument of the secular state, in which no religion is privileged, but must respect the religious convictions of all people.

4. The schools of Kenya must respect the cultural traditions of the peoples of Kenya, both as expressed in social institutions and relationships.

5. An excessively competitive spirit in our schools is incompatible with our traditional beliefs and must be restrained. Every young person coming from our schools must be made to realize that he has a valuable part to play in the national life.

6. Education must be regarded, and used as an instrument for the conscious change of attitudes and relationships, preparing children for those changes of outlook required by modern methods of productive organisations. At the same time, education must foster respect for human personality.

7. A most urgent objective of education is to sub-serve the needs of national development.
8. Education must promote social equality and remove divisions of race, tribe and religion. It must pay special attention to training in social obligation and responsibility.
9. An outcome to our education provision at all levels must be adaptability to change.

Recommendations of Ominde's Commission

The clear statement of the purpose of education apart, the commission made useful pragmatic recommendations regarding primary education, secondary education, commercial and technical education and adult education.

Concerning primary education, the commission stressed primary education as the state of acquiring foundation equipment for living. They wanted to see a primary school programme with emphasis on numeracy, literacy, and the rudiments of citizenship. They further urged a revision of syllabuses of Mathematics, Geography, English and History to make them Kenya-oriented. They advocated a new general science syllabus with Agriculture as part of it with an ample provision for the practical illustration of ideas, principles learnt in the classroom. They supported the existing arrangements for the control of primary schools by local authorities. The commission struck a new note when it recommended that no child should fail the Kenya Preliminary Examination (an exam at the end of primary school). Instead, certificates should be issued to all candidates, a certificate simply bearing results obtained. This was noteworthy reform for, each pupil would have something to show and would put an end to the 'failed K.P.E.' nonsense.

Turning to secondary education, the commission advocated for a policy to relate school output to the manpower needs in the areas of trade, industry and agriculture and, further stressed the importance of the practical aspects of the subjects taught. As no report on secondary education in East Africa would be complete without mention of examinations and school certificate, the commissioners suggested a general certificate of education showing passes obtained according to pupil's ability, and free from worry of whether he could meet the requirements for obtaining the school certificate.

The Ominde Commission also made significant recommendations concerning technical education which they wanted to see planned as a whole with close reference to ascertained demand for manpower. They charged the Ministry of Education with the responsibility to initiate the education and the training of Kenyans for industry, commerce and public service.

After the Ominde Commission

1. A Unified National Education System is Achieved

One of the tasks independent Kenyans had to perform after December 1963 was unifying the racially stratified education system of the colonial days into a national system. At first the task was somewhat difficult because former European and Asian schools charged much higher fees than the Kenyan pupil could afford. For this reason Ominde's Commission, as a long-term measure, recommended standardisation of rates of fees for all secondary schools. However, two measures helped to facilitate racial integration in secondary schools. (1) The government, through the Ministry of Education, gave bursaries to many deserving Kenyans and also paid grants to high-cost boarding secondary schools to enable them to remit the fees in the case of a deserving student. (2) From January 1967 the Ministry of Education ordered that from that year in all schools, any new intake must have at least 50 per cent Kenyans. By 1970 racial integration had been fully attained and some of the peculiar foreign names of schools had been Kenyanised. Also the Kenyanisation of secondary headships had gone a long way.

2. The Harambee School Movement Grows a pace

Harambee (self-help) secondary schools which derived their name from President Mzee Jomo Kenyatta's very effective rallying slogan "harambee" pulling together, were already in existence and in great numbers when Ominde and his team studied Kenya's educational system. Most of them hardly registered, and according to the letter of the law (Education Act) illegally established and operated, harambee schools formed one third of Kenya's secondary schools by 1965. The schools sprang up to absorb the enormous excess of primary school leavers after government secondary school intakes had been concluded. A harambee school invariably started with single streams forms I and 2.

The Ominde commission viewed the harambee school development with considerable trepidation and did not hesitate to make what now appears to have been a harsh recommendation. The commission said:

> We look with considerable anxiety on the present trend towards the creation of large numbers of small schools in Kenya and we urge that this trend immediately be arrested.

Indeed, in part two of their report (page 24) they further showed a surprisingly severe attitude to harambee schools:

> A project of this kind is well beyond the resources of most local communities...
> We consider it essential - for the sake of the spirit of self-help as much as for the sake of its objectives - that the impulse towards self-help should be diverted into the performance of tasks that lie within the capacity and resources of a community

to discharge successfully. In the education realm, such objectives can be found in primary education, in united contributions towards the buildings of maintained secondary schools, or in adult education projects.

It is hard to find grounds for sympathizing with the commission's anxiety. In fact, when the Ministry of Education tried to control the establishment of harambee secondary schools, it was opposed and its policy in regard to the subject described as 'imperialist', and government ministers and members of parliament went ahead to participate in the movement. Year after year more harambee schools have been opened and this has caused no regret or anxiety to the authorities. In fact, instead, gratitude has been expressed by government. For instance, the minister of education in 1968 stated:

> Without the harambee effort the rate of growth of secondary school places would not have grown as fast as it has. It is important to note that in spite of harambee effort, the country has no been able to provide enough secondary school places... the government has responded to and acknowledge this effort by working out a programme of assisting some of these schools with teachers by the beginning of 1969. *(Kenya Ministry of Education Annual Report, 1969).*

The harambee secondary school movement has over the years indicated Kenyans' enthusiasm and seriousness in regard to joint efforts for do-it-yourself educational projects. The harambee schools are now accepted as regular secondary education institutions and the authorities have virtually accepted responsibility over them.

3. The Rise in Number of the Developments at Aided Secondary Schools
One significant feature of post-independence educational development has been the enormous expansion of secondary education by the authorities. The magnitude of the expansion is impressively and vividly, portrayed by the following table:

	Aided Schools		Unaided Schools		Total	
Year	Schools	Pupils	Schools	Pupils	Schools	Pupils
1966	199	41,227	201	21,966	400	63,193
1967	206	49,488	336	39,291	542	88,779
1968	232	56,546	369	44,815	601	101,361
1969	263	65,644	431	49,602	694	115,246

It should be noted that the development of top forms of secondary schools have received special attention to meet manpower demands and to step up the number of university graduates. As elsewhere in East Africa, the appearance on the scene of huge numbers of secondary leavers unable to find jobs easily, has caused self-appointed critics to condemn the secondary school expansion.

Perhaps the presence of unemployed secondary leavers is better than a shortage of men with secondary education. The excess output of secondary schools is an achievement and not a problem. It need not depress us and it should be viewed as a potential source of wealth in human resources, awaiting exploitation as soon as means to do so become available.

Technical and commercial education too has received close attention and the developments in the two areas are astounding. Kenya Polytechnic, for example is the leading technical education institution. Note must be made of the now energetic move to set up through self-help what have been called institutes of technology in a number of areas. These institutions, other things being equal, are very likely to have a considerable impact in the field of education for industrial life.

4. Teacher Education

When Kenya gained her independence there were no less than 36 teacher training colleges, many of them small, understaffed, isolated, parochial in outlook and not likely to serve the independent nation's needs effectively. As funds became available, by a process of amalgamation, the number had by 1968 been reduced to 24 larger and more efficiently operated teacher education colleges. At the time of writing the number has been cut down to 17, but they have over 90,000 trainees in them.

The importance attached to teacher education was demonstrated when in 6-9 May 1968, a Conference to which top-level educational experts were invited from both inside and outside East Africa, was held in Nairobi.

As a result of the deliberations of the conference the steering committee of the board of delegates made recommendations on teacher education embodied in a document titled "New Directions in Teacher Education". The recommendations focused on two main objectives namely, the improvement of the quality of teacher education and producing effective well trained teachers for Kenya schools. Hence the committee recommended that tutors in teachers colleges be of graduate or graduate equivalent qualifications. Furthermore, principals should have not only excellent academic qualifications, but also appropriate experience and outstanding qualities of leadership and imagination. The aim should eventually be recruiting people with a minimum of 11 years of general education including four years at the secondary level. As a long-term policy, it was recommended that the teacher's certification should be approved by the highest academic institution in the country.

For effectiveness and efficiency the committee recommended that teachers colleges train two categories of teachers, that is primary school teachers and secondary school teachers. The 17 colleges already mentioned, have provisions to train primary school teachers for two years at three levels depending on the student's previous academic attainment.

For P 1 level, possession of the East African School Certificate (Kenya uses this certificate); then for P 2 at least two years of secondary education and for P 3, a Certificate of Primary Education (CPE) is adequate. It is important to point out that now that there are many East African School Certificate holders, it will no longer be necessary to have courses for P 2 and P 3 levels. In fact, it is planned (1973) to arrange for the Form Two level teachers, now numbering 2,000, to undergo in-service training so that they may be up-graded. It appears that it is no longer necessary to accept holders of the CPE for training as teachers.

Secondary school teachers who are non-graduates and who referred to as S-1, have been trained at Kenyatta College (now a university college of Kenyatta University) since 1964, and Kenya Science Teachers College since 1966. In 1972 Kenyatta College became Kenyatta University College and enrolled 200 undergraduates straight away. In 1973, in all, the college has 600 students reading for the degree and will take up teaching on graduation.

The department of education which was established at the University of Nairobi in 1966 (then a university college) to offer graduate studies in education has now grown into a faculty of education. Today it offers undergraduate and post graduate courses for students in preparation for a teaching career.

5. Administration, Control and Supervision
Since independence the Minister with the assistance of two Assistant Ministers appointed by the President has been in charge of the Ministry of Education. Since 1968, by an Act of Parliament it is his duty:

> To promote the education of the people of Kenya and the progressive development of institutions devoted to the promotion of such education, and to secure the effective co-operation under his general direction or control, of all public bodies concerned with education in carrying out the national policy for education.

Thus through him the government had full responsibility for all education. The Education Act 1968, which has already been mentioned, brought up to date all education legislation and regulations previously made and clearly laid down the legal framework within which local authorities and boards of governors were to carry out duties assigned to them. The Act made legal provisions concerning the registration of unaided schools, inspection and control of schools, examinations and diplomas, Kenya Institute of Education and use of public funds by the minister in order to promote education.

The Act further conferred powers on the minister in the exercise of which he has made the Education (school committees) Regulations 1968, the Education (Entrustment of functions to Local Authorities) Order 1968, which delegated certain duties to Local Authorities, the education (Board of Governors) Order 1969 by virtue of which the Minister appoints the chairman of the board and has authorised Kianda College to issue certificates or diplomas to its students. At the time of writing this account the main officers in the civil servant team responsible for the day-to-day huge duties involved in administering Kenya's education system at the headquarters are as follows: permanent secretary - the ministry's senior civil servant and its chief administrator, director of education, deputy secretary, chief inspector of schools, deputy director of education, assistant director of education and senior examination officers. In the field are provincial education officers and district education officers.

25

Uganda

Uganda government takes positive steps to control and Administer Education Effectively

Castle Education Commission 1963

After Uganda had gained her independence in 1962, a commission under the chairmanship of Professor E. B. Castle, formerly professor of education at Hull University, was appointed in 1963 to report on education in Uganda with the following terms of reference:

> To examine in the light of the approved recommendations of the International Bank Survey Mission Report and Uganda's financial position and future manpower requirements, the content and structure of education in Uganda; to consider how it may be improved and adapted to the needs of this country and to submit recommendations accordingly.

The commission which had the service of a number of outstanding Ugandan men of learning, addressed themselves with considerable insight to the exacting task of visualising the needs of an independent state and recommending a school structure to meet these needs.

Some of the needs were indicated and stressed in the memoranda received by the commission, from people who had reflected on the system of education as it was before independence and found it inadequate and not likely to be suitable to an independent nation. To use one of the many memoranda the commission received, a Uganda lecturer in Economics at Makerere University College in memorandum called for the education system to be put on a scientific basis. Spelling out this statement, he had this to say:

> The only way Uganda can decolonise her educational system is to place emphasis on science. The country can not afford to base its system on outmoded irrelevant and traditional definitions of education. Physical training, spiritual training and character building are the very things that have drawn education in Uganda into a stalemate and resulting in the bulk of its products thinking of themselves as 'superior and religious' and unwilling to do technical and manual work. The products of technical schools and colleges dotted about Uganda do not cater for the real technical requirements of the country.

Although no educator in the real sense would regard physical training and character building as irrelevant in education, and although the lecturer did not indicate how the system of education could be put on a scientific basis as he advocated, he at least certainly put his dissatisfaction with the colonial system of education in bold terms. Many other people were in the same way critical of the system.

The memorandum submitted to the commission did not only criticise the school curriculum but its organisation as well. A Ugandan teachers' union, Mbale Region, told the commission that all the schools must be nationalised or controlled by the state government, adding that the system as it existed then hindered good teachers from one denominational school from going to teach in another. The commission, therefore, did its work in circumstances where there was an expressed need for change in the system.

Castle Education Commission Recommendations

The commission made the following main recommendations:-
1. Primary school course to last seven years instead of eight.
2. A revision of the primary syllabus to be undertaken so as to produce pupils better prepared for life and future study than hitherto.
3. That there should be established four types of post-primary institutions to admit a proportion of primary school leavers.
    (a) High schools – offering an academic course, although some of them could have a technical bias.
    (b) Secondary schools – to offer general and vocational education.
    (c) Technical schools – to conduct a four-year course leading to City and Guilds Examination.
    (d) Farm Schools – to conduct a four-year course.

The Castle Commission Report's most significant element was its wise and searching analysis and comments on purely educational matters. Its main shortcoming, however, was that there was no indication of the financial and manpower implications of the vast recommendations made. It may also be added that the commission's suggestion that concentration be on increasing the quality of primary education, in circumstances where many primary school-age pupils had no opportunity to go to school, just could not be acceptable.

The government fortunately decided to increase both quality and quantity of primary education. The publication of the Castle Report was followed by the publication of Government's Sessional Paper No. 4 of 1963 in which the Government set out its policy on the report in particular and in general. At the same time the Education (Amendment) Act 1963 was enacted to enable the Central Government, as it was called then, to secure sufficient control over all details of educational planning and development throughout the country.

Problems Encountered and Solved in the Process of Creating a National Education System After the Castle Report

Responsibility and Control

The Castle Report assigned the responsibility for education in Uganda to the central and local governments. However, on the question of control only three of the members of the commission expressed the view that this should belong to the central and local governments too. It seemed thus, by implication, that the control and supervision of schools was believed by the majority of the commissioners not to belong to voluntary agencies. In one of the longest debates on education in parliament here, the government made it absolutely clear that the voluntary agencies would hencefourth not control schools. The government was, instead going to control schools.

Up to 1963, some post-primary institutions, secondary schools, teacher training colleges, technical schools and, the greatest number of primary schools (except a few in urban areas), were administered and managed on a religious denominational basis by voluntary agencies. The voluntary agencies were Catholic missions, the Uganda Muslim Education Association and Protestant missions.

It is true that there were a number of inter-denominational primary schools founded by the local and central governments just as there were inter-denominational secondary schools again founded by the central government, but we think it is safe to say that their number was small. Each of the three voluntary agencies had an educational secretary general with his headquarters in Kampala. Under each educational secretary general, each voluntary agency had, wherever possible, for each district or every two districts, a school supervisor with several assistants and auxiliary clerical and accountancy staff. With this administrative set-up, the voluntary agencies had a considerable amount of control in the schools, particularly to the extent that they decided who should be admitted, who should teach there and who should be a headmaster. It was, under the system as it existed, unthinkable for a Catholic to head a Protestant school or for a Muslim to head any of the Christian voluntary agencies' schools. For many years there had been intensive rivalry among voluntary agencies in setting up schools in many parts of the country. Except for a few foundations which trace their beginnings back to the early 1920s, for example Kibuli School, the Uganda Muslim Education Association had come late into the field of setting up schools, but was doing well by 1963. The Muslim agency had many schools although not as many as each of the other agencies had.

The system was particularly wasteful of the country's limited resources; For instance, the use of three supervisors in an area where one supervisor would have been adequate; or half-empty schools caused by not having enough pupils of the faith which the voluntary agency represented. It was not unusual for a pupil to walk past a school near his home to a distant school because that was the institution managed by his denomination (where he would be acceptable).

In 1964, the government abolished the posts of educational secretaries general, education secretaries and school supervisors and after this, all matters concerning primary and junior secondary schools were centralised in the education office. Except in Buganda where the then Kabaka's (kings) government obliquely controlled some secondary schools until 1966, all secondary schools in the country came under the direct control of the central government in 1964.

Re-organisation of Administration and Control of Schools and the Integration of Religious Education Systems

To implement the changes already mentioned first, at least 54 assistant education officers were appointed for work in area education offices. Secondly, the chief education officer was given powers to require a teacher to serve in any school in Uganda, and to retire teachers.

The implementation of the re-organisation of the administration and the control of schools was not accepted without criticism and resistance and this made 1964 a difficult year for the Ministry of Education. Criticism inside parliament aside, there was sharp open criticism of the new education policy outside. For example, the *Uganda Argus* newspapers of Tuesday, 16 January, 1964, reported that the Uganda Vernacular, primary, and junior teachers' union had passed resolutions expressing concern over the government's "dictatorial action" of taking over schools without the consent and agreement of the owners. One of the main arguments put forward by the leaders of the resistance, where it occurred, was that ownership of the school buildings (voluntary agencies claimed ownership of school buildings) could not be separated from the administration and control of the schools.

Resistance in at least one part of the country was real and it became necessary to meet it with drastic measures. For instance in Buganda, the then minister of education in the then Kabaka's government, had stated in February 1964 that according to the new education policy heads of schools were required to collect school fees and bank it into a specific bank account through the district education office. However, it was found out in March that some schools were not doing this. The *Uganda Argus* of Tuesday, 5 March reported the Kabaka's government reaction to this act of disobedience to the declared policy, embodied in a statement, from the Buganda ministry of education office, which read:

> Government grants have been withdrawn from 19 Catholic schools whose owners have refused to hand their fees to district education officers in accordance with the new education policy.

When in June the Uganda minister of education, after referring to the incidents of resistance in Buganda, told parliament that he would introduce rules and amendments to the Education Act 1963 to enable government's education policy to be enforced, there ensued a battle of words outside parliament. On 11 July, 1964, at a large outdoor meeting in Kampala, self-appointed spokesmen of the resistance called for the resignation of the minister of education. Some of them suggested in speech that the new education policy marked the beginning of Communism.

Despite all the bickerings and resistance which eventually, came to nought the government continued to stress that tribalism and religious sectionalism had no place in Uganda's new educational system, and before long the integration of the separate racial and religious systems of education was accomplished.

Problem of Staffing Secondary Schools and Financing the Expansion of Secondary Education

On King's College Budo's speech day, Saturday 25 July, 1964 the expatriate headmaster Mr. Ian Robinson, told the parents and all guests:

> Until Uganda can produce enough of her own teachers, schools are going to be difficult to run because expatriates are nowadays birds of passage staying one or two tours ... Staffing and money are big problems in school administration.

Robinson certainly knew what he was talking about and he was right.

In 1964 secondary schools were and have until recently been staffed mainly by expatriates through schemes, namely: the Teachers for East Africa initiated in 1961; the Teacher Education East; Peace Corps U.S.A.; and Volunteer Service Overseas, Britain, Germany and Norway. At the same time the British Department of Technical Co-operation recruited teachers for East Africa. In 1964 there were no more than 40 Uganda graduates teaching in secondary schools and teacher training colleges and the rest were expatriates. Lack of an adequate local source of graduate teachers made maintenance and expansion of secondary school education difficult and expensive. The expansion required sums of money which were not in the country's budget. Hence it became necessary to get loans to carry it out. Sources of loans were in the early days, U.S.A., Britain and the World Bank. Other sources have since 1964 been found.

The Ministry of Education, when announcing in 1964 the opening of Tororo Girls' School in 1965 and extensions to Budo, Tororo, Lango, and Butobere through an American loan, pointed out that there were two difficulties ahead (i) the procurement of supplies from U.S.A. (one of the loan conditionalities) and (ii) provision of about £500,000 being the annual opening costs of those schools. The point we are trying to drive home here is that secondary school expansion particularly, has been very expensive and a great deal of facilities have been made available through foreign loans which sometimes had strings attached.

No effort our expense has been spared to expand secondary education since 1962. Enrolment per class has been raised from 25 pupils in the protectorate days, to 40 pupils after independence. Some schools operate a system known as "double session," where half the school uses facilities in the morning and another one in the afternoon. Thus, it has been possible to have a school with 2,000 pupils on the register. Teaching loads have also increased. In boarding schools double deck-beds were introduced. Quite often critics say that there was no planning. Maybe they are right, but the nation had an emergency on its hands, namely, to produce the manpower required urgently and there was no time for detailed planning based on carefully constructed formulae. That the system has not collapsed because of pressures and strain it has been subjected to, is in itself an achievement.

A number of schemes to step up the number of teachers for secondary schools have been undertaken, for instance the turning of Kyambogo from a Grade III teachers college to the status of a national teachers' college training non-graduate teachers for work the secondary schools. To this has been added the up-grading to secondary teacher status, primary school teachers for upper classes through a short course at the Institute of Education. Makerere started a Bachelor of Education course in 1963 which was phased out in 1971 and then began provisions whereby a student took a degree in any discipline while at the same time he or she underwent training as a teacher, so that in three academic years, he has a degree as well as a teaching qualification.

At present about 600 students are registered and they make use of the arrangement. This should go along way in giving schools local graduate teachers.

The Problem of Allocating Places in Secondary Schools

Since 1964 the Ministry of Education has had to supervise the selection of pupils for government aided secondary schools. The selection is based on merit in the Primary Leaving Examination. The headteachers meet in one place in Kampala for a week to carry out the exercise under the close supervision of the chief education officer or his representative. The reason for this is not because headteachers can not do the selection at their own schools, but because by doing it in one place, it might be ensured that all places available have been correctly and fairly filled. The exercise ensures that the best pupils get good places at the secondary schools where places are few and open to stiff academic competition. The arrangement makes it difficult for the rejection of a pupil by a headteacher on grounds other than lack of merit. At the selection meeting reasons for rejecting a candidate must be given openly for everybody present to hear. Where the reason is not convincing, the chief education officer rules that the candidate be accepted.

Private Secondary Schools Since Independence

Each year the number of primary school leavers seeking secondary school education has exceeded the number of places available at government-aided secondary schools. For those not selected, private schools have sprung up like mushrooms to offer them secondary education. There has been a variety of such schools, and indeed some of them are not worth calling secondary schools, for they are no where near the required standard in terms of buildings, teaching personnel or even headship. Their operators are out to make money with the minimum of services given to pupils.

Although the Ministry of Education has not prohibited the opening up of private schools, it has from time to time intervened to help, to advise and check on what is going on. A report on private schools in 1969 listed 23 private secondary schools which had been registered by the ministry and recognised for presenting candidates for the East African Certificate of Education (EACE) exams. Sixty nine had been registered by the ministry but ineligible for presenting candidates for the EACE exams. Eleven were on the waiting list for registration and 6 commercial schools had been registered by Ministry of Education and 204 as 'deplorable' and unregistered.

In the same report suggestions were made for those intending to open private schools, about cost and other requirements. The report suggested that the initial cost of starting one class of 40 pupils was shs. 23,000 plus shs. 500 a year as fees for recurrent expenditure, if no boarding facilities were needed. For opening a four-class boarding school, the capital needed for 160 pupils would be shs. 140,000 with recurrent expenditure being met from fees at the rate of shs. 1,100 a year paid by each pupil.

It was also suggested that 25 per cent of the teaching staff should be registered teachers. It seems the advice was not taken notice of so that the 1970 Education Act made special provisions relating to a private school. They were all intended to make the establishing of a private school an unattractive enterprise. The law made the process one has to go through in order to establish a private school lengthy, tedious and costly. It empowers the chief education officer to classify the school when all conditions as laid down in the Act are satisfied. It requires registration of private schools. Even change of ownership of a private school needs the approval of the chief education officer. The Act further gave the minister powers to fix fees at any private school. Contravention of the law is punishable by a fine of Shs. 6,000 for first offence, a term of imprisonment for a second time of conviction.

Asians, while they were still many in the country, turned private schools operation into quick money making business. They employed teachers with poor academic background although on the official register they had names of teachers duly qualified but were never in school. One individual had a chain of private schools.

Grappling With the Subject of Curriculum Reform

Primary School Curriculum

"If you want to reform curriculum, change the syllabuses," it has been suggested. When the Castle Commission reported on education in Uganda in 1963, subject panels were already busy revising syllabuses in order to have a new primary school syllabus that would suit Uganda. The new syllabus first appeared in 1965. In its introductory pages it was stated:

> This syllabus has been drawn up by subject panels constituted by the Advisory Committee for Teacher Training. These panels have consisted of teachers, teacher trainers, inspectors of schools and members of the Institute of Education, Makerere. Their work has been co-ordinated by the Advisory Committee and in its final stages by the Chief Inspector of Schools.

Thus the new syllabus was the work of educational experts: Giving reasons for the production of a new syllabus it was stated:

> A new nation requires a new outlook on the teaching of many school subjects. The syllabus must be geared to the needs of the school leavers in the new society and must also attempt to indicate to children their place as citizens of Uganda and of Africa. The new syllabus, particularly in Science, History/Civics and Geography reflects these changes.

Produced by experts, with reasons for its introduction clearly stated, and advice on how to use it given, the new syllabus was in its content a satisfactory indication that effort was being made through a broader programme to cater for childhood in Uganda's primary schools. To ensure that teachers use it effectively, in service training programmes were organised and operated and are still going on. However, about 3 years after its introduction, its use was made difficult by measures made on sometimes political grounds or on grounds made necessary by a desire to keep within financial limits. The policy of centralised production and marketing of educational materials severely limited the source of books and scholastic materials to use in implementation of the syllabus.

For example, there were books listed as essential in the syllabus but in fact unavailable because they were not yet published. The central organisation, managed and directed by expatriates, which was given the task of producing books written by Ugandans, on several occasions received manuscripts but did not publish them, or when it did, it was already too late to use the books. Pupils had moved into another form. The organisation set up to supply and sell scholastic materials just could not cope with the task which was too big for it and for which not much preparation had been done before operation started.

Delays in delivery and non-delivery became a daily experience for teachers. The situation has of late improved and the syllabus which is still in force can be implemented with some ease now. However, its impact remains to be measured by means other than the present Primary Leaving Examination.

Secondary School Curriculum

Although there was much talk about the need for changes in secondary school curriculum for three years after independence no attempt was made to translate this into action. There were reasons for this, for example shortage of teachers and facilities. Castle's suggestion that schools with agricultural or technical biases be set up, was being implemented but there was no clear statement on what their curriculum would be like.

In November 1965, however, the then chief inspector of schools, the first Ugandan to hold that position, sent out to heads of secondary schools a document comprising proposals about the subjects to be taken in the secondary school programme and invited comments. The immediate reaction to the document by people, who one would expect to be responsive to curriculum proposals, was unduly discouraging and obstructive. The simple explanation for the secondary school heads' reaction is that, it seemed to them that the proposals would effect the look of the overall results of a given school. This would especially be so when a pupil in S4 would take 8 subjects in the Cambridge School Certificate Examination. Those were days when heads of schools, understandably, attached importance to a school's performance in the Cambridge School Certificate Examinations. They were very much encouraged in this by the publicity given to a school's Cambridge exams results in the newspaper media, which often had statements such as "School C has so many first grades and no third grades." Many schools, it must be pointed out, in a drive to enable their pupils to get grade I certificates, allowed early meaningless specialisation. Some pupils were allowed to leave out subjects they felt they were not good at and concentrate on only 6 subjects for two years, finally ending with a grade I certificate but based on a narrow curriculum. The Cambridge Exams Syndicate required a good overall performance in 6 subjects selected from groups laid down in its regulations, to award a grade I certificate. Some pupils dropped Mathematics or Geography or Physical Science or History in Senior 2. Practical subjects were often left out. The public judged schools in terms of Cambridge School Certificate results. Remarks that a certain school had good results and was therefore a good school, were often heard.

The chief inspector of schools, determined that there should be changes in the secondary school curriculum, after talks with heads of schools and correspondence with them for a number of months. He issued a final circular on secondary school curriculum in August 1966 with clear indication that all aided secondary schools would be required to follow it. The heads of schools (mostly expatriates) now saw no point in not accepting the proposals and they now concentrated on persuading the inspectorate to consider certain modifications in it. The chief inspector's proposals from the start of the secondary school curriculum campaign were aimed, as he explained, at broadening pupils' general education that would provide a grounding for higher studies and preparation for adult life.

In addition to traditional academic subjects, the proposals included practical subjects the teaching of which the ministry would make provisions for. Since 1967, secondary school curriculum for a normal secondary school, at Senior 4 level consists of (i) a core of subjects all pupils must do and these are: English, Biology, Mathematics, Geography, History and Physical Science (ii) one subject selected by the pupil from a group comprising practical land commercial skill subjects, and (iii) one subject selected from a group comprising languages and religious knowledge subjects.

To enforce this, the ministry has since 1969 required all Senior 4 candidates for the East African Certificate of Education Examinations which have taken the place of the former Cambridge School Certificate exams to sit for eight subjects, and strictly in line with the prescribed curriculum. Furthermore, to get all pupils to toe the line, the selection for Higher School Certificate courses has been and is based on overall satisfactory performance in 8 subjects. Surprisingly, the curriculum has caused no disaster and as there are no classified certificates in the E.A.C.E. exams, there is now no ill-feeling towards it. Indeed, many secondary schools have happily embraced the new approach to the teaching of Maths and Science and have gladly accepted revised syllabuses in History and Geography.

Makerere University's Faculty of Education, Kyambogo National Teachers College and a core of secondary school teachers in the field, have contributed considerably to curriculum development and implementation. Meanwhile, The East African Examinations Council has shown much willingness to set exams on any syllabus brought to its notice in time. Much still remains to be done in the area of curriculum development and reconstruction, although effort still continues.

The Boom in Secondary School Education

Curriculum changes apart, there are two important things to note about secondary education in the period under review. Firstly, the integration of the separate racial and religious systems, which were a main feature of education before 1962, has now been completed. A child can gain admission to any school irrespective of his race or religion and without fear that he will be compelled to undergo religious instruction in order to keep his place in the school.

Secondly, there has been an expansion in facilities for secondary education to an extent unheard of and never even expected before independence. As a result, many girls and boys have been offered the opportunity of secondary school education. The tables given below show the magnitude of the numbers of those who have benefited from secondary school education at aided schools in the period 1963-1968:

Year	Intake S1	Total output S4	Total enrolment S1-4
1963	3067	1907	9,542
1964	4100	2068	11,709
1965	6106	2499	16,709
1966	6504	3029	20,003
1967	8468	4239	25,180
1968	9085	5936	30,026

Higher School Certificate

Year	Intake S5	Output S6	Total enrolment S5-6
1963	399	254	653
1964	575	368	943
1965	608	523	1,131
1966	966	579	1,545
1967	941	904	1,845
1968	1,290	932	2,222

The figures in the above tables do not include the numbers of pupils at what are known as private schools of which there are many.

Teacher Education

In the area of teacher education it had been planned in 1965 to absorb all the existing primary teachers colleges into four large regional teachers colleges built in four carefully selected places but it has not been possible to do this. Instead, it is planned to expand 10 of the existing colleges in the period 1974-80 so that each can initially take 135 students but later on raise the enrolment to 500 students.

Some of the main suggestions made since 1971 which, if implemented, are very likely to give rise to valuable educational changes to teacher education are briefly as follows:-

1. Teacher training colleges currently (1973) training primary teachers be developed into 500-student colleges of education with tremendous emphasis on quality in their programmes of teacher education.

2. National Teachers College Kyambogo to-date training non graduate teachers for secondary schools, turn to
   (a) running in-service education courses for secondary school teachers.
   (b) training teachers for special areas, e.g. agriculture and design.
   (c) mounting degree courses with due regard to needs of teachers.
3. The Curriculum Development Centre concentrates on curriculum development and production of teaching materials.
4. The Institute of Education (in existence since 1964), and now mainly conducting primary teacher training colleges programmes, exams, up-grading of tutors establishes,
   (a) education section to cater for
      (i) pre-school and primary education;
      (ii) special education;
      (iii) in-service education for primary teachers and;
   (b) a teacher education department;
      (i) to conduct in-service courses for teacher educators;
      (ii) to provide or help provide materials for teachers.
5. The Faculty of Education at Makerere University now training graduate teachers and conducting research and guiding studies for higher degrees in education, develops
   (a) emphasis on curriculum development for the secondary school (in conjunction with Curriculum Development Centre).
   (b) department of educational management for
      (i) studies and research in educational administration and management of schools,
      (ii) in-service education,
      (iii) course work towards higher degrees in education,
   (c) a working relation with the Centre for Continuing Education at Makerere in an area of out of school education and training adult educators.
6. The Ministry of Education, in addition to its administration and finance functions,
   (i) to strengthen the professional standing of teacher educators by the creation of posts of assistant chief education officer and assistant chief inspector of schools and colleges-for teacher education,
   (ii) to help the administration of colleges of education by more generous provision of non-teaching staff and more funds.
      The other suggestion made which we would like to mention is the establishment of a school of education whose nature and function is still being debated.

Finally, technical education has received more attention than the period before 1963. The Uganda Technical College, the apex of technical education here, until 1967 accepted students for undergraduate level engineering courses which were completed at Srathclyde University in Scotland, which were suspended in 1968, for active preparation was being made to start degree-level work in engineering at Makerere. Technician and crafts courses have however continued and with the assistance of a team of UNESCO specialists, the college has trained a good number of engineering technicians. At the same time, some of the Ugandan lecturers have been given fellowships for further study overseas in the United Kingdom so that they can take over from the UNESCO team.

By the end of 1967 there were five technical schools with an enrolment of 1,177 students on the following courses: boat-building, block-laying and concrete practice, carpentry and joinery, electrical installations, machine shop engineering, motor vehicle mechanics, painting and decorating, plumbing, and gin-fitting. All these are obviously useful courses for making available technicians with skills often called for in many areas of activity.

At the time of writing proposals have reached an advanced form for raising the standards of entry into technical institutions, for updating the courses they offer, and for the Uganda Technical College to play an even bigger role in producing more and more men with technical know-how to meet the manpower requirements that have been thrust on the country by the technological age we live in.

Courses in business studies are now conducted at a high level in the Uganda Business School of Makerere University based at the Nakawa campus which used to house the Uganda College of Commerce. The business school now offers a variety of courses, some leading to the award of master's degrees. Long ago the site used to be an engineering school for a short period in the Protectorate days.

26

Tanganyika (Tanzania After 1964)

Launching the Three-Year Education Plan 1962

The task facing independent Tanganyika was the further development of education that the challenge of independence called for. Two things indicated the seriousness and resolution with which the Tanganyikans meant to tackle the task.

Firstly, a 3-year plan was drawn up in 1961 and launched on January 1962, with development focused on the following subjects:

1. Expansion of secondary school facilities as a priority. The desired target of expansion was expressed clearly in figures. Efforts were to be made to raise the number of School Certificate candidates from 1,398 in 1961 to 3,275 in 1964, and the number of Higher School Certificate candidates from 168 in 1961 to 620 in 1964.
2. Making additional facilities available for the expansion and improving of teacher training courses at post-primary and post-secondary level. This was important as no educational expansion can ever be achieved without an increased number of teachers.
3. Expansion of facilities at the Dar-es-Salaam Technical College and opening classes in two centres outside Dar.
4. Expansion of the primary school course from 4 to 6 years. It was also intended to make it an 8-year course later, thus absorbing the middle schools.

The 3-year plan was warmly welcomed by the Tanganyika National Assembly and the comments and observations by members present, leave no shed of doubt in one's mind as to what independent Tanganyikans wanted the education system to accomplish. Most speakers were emphatic in waiting to see the school system play a major role in nation building. Although it was realised that it would not be possible to have a secondary school in every district, and much as what the government proposed to do was appreciated, members of the assembly expressed the hope that setting up more secondary schools would be undertaken. The government's approach was bold but this was only a beginning.

The question of use of Kiswahili instead of English in schools of all levels was brought up. One member who suggested that it was not true Kiswahili was a very narrow language, advised the minister of education to set up a machinery so that in the long run all teaching could be conducted in it, in all schools.

The discussion on the use of Kiswahili in schools so as to give the country a national language, and a revision of the syllabus, plus proposals of an accelerated programme for training locally, teachers for Tanganyika schools went on. But it was shown that the Tanganyikans wanted a national programme of education and this also foreshadowed the programme of education for self-reliance with which Tanzania is now associated.

1962 Education Ordinance Integrates Education System

In October 1961, a new education ordinance was made to commence operation on 1 January 1962. It marked the beginning of a new era in education in Tanganyika. It made four important provisions:

1. From the 1 January, 1962, there was to be a single system of education instead of the three separate racial systems. All schools were to be open to any person irrespective of race or religion as long as he was qualified in the normal way as applicable to all candidates. There was now going to be one policy for the entire system of education in the country, and the minister of education explained on the occasion of the second reading of the bill before it became law, the proposed expenditure for education had been based on a single system. For this provision particularly, the enactment of the measure that would take the nation a long way towards unity. There was no lack of evidence that the country as a whole, for this provision, welcomed the ordinance.
2. From the beginning of the new year, local authorities were going to be responsible for primary education. Local authorities meant municipal councils, district councils, town councils and native authority as established by appropriate ordinances. Under this provision, the Local authority concerned would discharge a number of responsibilities among which were the preparation and submission for approval of annual budget for education, receiving and administration of grants-in-aid from public funds, advising the minister of education on ownership and registration of new schools, enforcement of compulsory attendance as the minister of Education might direct under the provisions of the ordinance.

    The degree of decentralisation of the administration of primary school education made possible by the ordinance was given welcome by the members of the assembly.
3. (a) boards of governors for post-primary institutions would be set up by the minister and would manage schools or groups of schools.
    (b) school committees were to be set up.
4. The chief education officer was empowered to classify schools depending on level and nature of education provided therein.
5. The ordinance decreed that no school could be established or run unless,
    (a) the minister had prior to this approved "owner" as the owner of that type of school,

(b) the manager of the school had been approved as manager of the school by the chief education officer,

(c) the school is registered as required under the ordinance,

(d) all teaching staff had been registered as teachers.

Control would thus become tighter than previous ordinances had decreed.

With a comprehensive plan and an ordinance, a good start was made in 1962. If progress can be measured by rising enrolment, the number of institutions established and increase in types of final products, then the following figures prepared by the Ministry of Education and presented at the end of 1964, tell an impressive story.

Year	1962	1963	1964
Primary	518,663	592,104	710,200
Secondary	14,175	17,077	19,897

Education for Self-Reliance

One feature of educational development since independence is that it focuses on a clearly stated objective and within the prescriptions of a political ideology which guides the authorities and indeed people under them for all aspects of development of a socialist society. Education is for self-reliance. It is a radical programme, drawn up, initiated and directed closely by the authorities. According to the programme, Mwalimu Julius Kambarage Nyerere suggested:

> Each school should have, as an integral part of it, a farm or workshop which provides the food eaten by the community, and makes some contribution to the total national income. This is not attached to every school for training purposes. It is a suggestion that every school should also be a farm; that the school community should consist of people who are both teachers and farmers and pupils and farmers.

Those charged with the implementation of the programme have had to go through the motions of a complete rethinking and a difficult exercise. Since 1967, one no longer talks of education but of national education and hence the Ministry of National Education. Some of the highlights of the programme have been:

(a) the attempt to use Kiswahili as a medium of instruction throughout the primary schools since 1967, English being taught as a subject. It would be dishonest to say there have been no difficulties. There have been difficulties but luckily this time there are no foreigners or colonialists to suspect of being obstructive, the *Wanainchi* have to address themselves to the task and they are doing so,

(b) the abolition of examinations for secondary school leavers set and marked outside Tanzania

(c) a declaration of free primary education, August 1973.

27

Higher Education 1922-1970

Makerere University

When in March 1929, the directors of education held their annual conference in Dar-es-Salaam, they agreed unanimously that higher education for East Africans should be centred at Makerere, Kampala. Makerere had been in existence, providing higher education than any other institution, for at least seven years. While it had started as a technical school it had in a fairly short time embarked with considerable success on courses in Medicine, Agriculture, Elementary Engineering, Surveying and Teacher education. Besides these professional courses, a general education programme was run which by 1935 led to the award of the Cambridge School Certificate. From its early days, Makerere College as it was known, was held in high esteem and the training it offered made a mark on its students.

In 1935 the secretary of state for the colonies appointed a commission to examine and report on higher education in East Africa. The commission arrived in East Africa in January 1937 with the following as members:- The Right Hon. Earl de la Warr (chairman); Mr Robert Bernays , MP; Miss Phillipa Esdaile, D.Sc.; Mr B. Mowat Jones, DSO, MA; Dr Alexander Kerr, MA, LL.D; Dr WH. McLean, Ph.D, M. Inst., CE; Mr Z.K. Mathews, MA.; LL.B; Dr John Murray, MA, LL.D; The Hon Harold Nicholson, CMG., MP; Mr F.J. Pedler, Colonial Office (Secretary). Obviously, there was no Ugandan in the team nor was there an East African and there is no evidence to show that there was no such person suitable for serving on the commission.

The commission was asked to examine and report on the organisation and working of Makerere College and to make recommendations of its development and administration. The commission was also to study and report on institutions or other agencies for vocational training connected with Makerere College. The educational system of the territories from which the college drew its students were to be studied and reported on. In making recommendations, the commission was asked to consider carefully the general interest and needs of the communities from which future students might be drawn and the education needs of the women.

The commission carried out their mission with considerable zeal and made many long-sighted recommendations. They stressed relevance of the education programme to the environment and called for improvement and expansion of primary education. They did not forget to associate this with proper training and better pay for primary teachers. The commission recommended improvement of existing secondary schools. The need for an East African School Leaving Examination was emphasised, that should be based on a syllabus suited in content to African conditions but at a standard comparable to that of examinations recognised by British examining bodies. The commission wanted the education of girls to be developed as a matter of prime urgency, with stress on training for home making. The appointment of a director of women's education was strongly recommended.

As far as Makerere College was directly concerned, the following specific recommendations were made:-

1. All post-secondary courses at the college and its associated institutions to form the Higher College of East Africa.
2. The principal and staff of the Higher College to be university type and of University status.
3. The Higher College should award its own diplomas and efforts be made to secure recognition of these diplomas by universities and professional bodies.
4. The Higher College should have an autonomous governing body.
5. Continuation of professional courses in teacher education, Medicine, Agriculture and Veterinary Science was recommended.
6. The Higher College to be a centre for research and to maintain contact with other research institutions.
7. Suitable students who completed courses at the Higher College should be encouraged to continue studies outside East Africa and the government should state their policy regarding the employment of Africans with post-secondary education.

An international conference held in 1938 to consider the commission's recommendations accepted in general the outline of the Higher College's structure as suggested by the commission. The Makerere College Ordinance of 1938 created an assembly for the college, and the Makerere College Council. In 1938 a new principal arrived and the use of lectures and tutorials, instead of lessons and classes, and the abolition of roll calls, the prefect system and compulsory physical education were some indications (to students particularly) that Makerere had now ceased to be a senior secondary school and was heading for university status.

For the next six years, 1939-1945, progress was slow obviously because of the war. However, construction of buildings went on and the main building, now the central administration block, and the two chapels were ready in 1941.

There was curtailment in every field and the council endeavoured to effect strict economy of available resources. In passing it may be mentioned that the year 1940 saw the end of the engineering course, as it had become impossible to recruit staff. The number of students at the college continued to be small (standing at 181) which included 28 Kenyans, 31 Tanganyikans and 9 Zanzibarians in 1940.

The Road to the Status of University College 1945-60

Despite considerable setbacks caused by the war, the council made plans for the college to conduct academic courses which were not linked to professional training, and to make provisions for the academic staff to undertake research and, wherever possible, to involve able students. To implement this, higher courses in Science and Arts were started in 1944. The Vice-Principal Mr. T.R. Batten, M.A. (Oxon), added something interesting to the curriculum. Every registered student, Science or Arts, did a one-year Social Studies course which attempted to make him aware of East Africa's economic and social problems. There was also a compulsory one-year English language course for all except English majors. All these courses aimed at providing a broad general background to professional training and were conducted at post-School Certificate level although for some unknown reason not very many students passed the examinations at the end of the course.

In 1945, the Commission of Higher Education in the Colonies, the Asquith Commission, visiting Makerere, observed and reported that in the period since the de la Warr Commission of 1937, the college had taken creditable steps towards becoming a university through the first stage of a university college. In general, their report had a favourable, positive tone and encouraged Makerere to continue in the same direction.

But Makerere could not move fast. Although the war was over and there was a new principal, Dr. D. Lamont, formerly professor of Moral Philosophy, Cairo University, there were some difficulties such as the delivery of equipment badly needed was still slow; staff recruitment presented problems as academic opportunities and salary scales existing then were not attractive enough to lure university teachers.

Inspite of these difficulties, determined that the college should develop further, the East African High Commission (the three governors) assented to the Makerere College Act on 24 February 1949. The Act made a provision for government control and administration of Makerere College. Under the Act a council of 14 members under the chairmanship of Sir R.E. Robins, C.M.G., O.B.E., was set up. Surprisingly there was no African on it and there can be no acceptable explanation for this as there were a few eligible Africans.

Soon after the Makerere College Act, the Inter-University Council despatched delegates to conduct on-the-spot discussions on the future development of the college. The delegates, five in number and all of them experienced university teachers and administrators, together with the Makerere Academic Board, after long discussions came out with a plan, subject to the approval of London University, to enable students to read for external degrees of the University of London. London University accepted the proposals and degree courses started in March 1950. The delegates and Makerere lecturers suggested that for the time being the requirements for admission to the degree course would be a pass in a test of competence in English Language plus a number of credits at School Certificate Examinations. The first two years (equivalent of A-level) would be spent preparing student candidates for London University Intermediate Examinations.

The intermediate course started in March 1950 with a group that not only had passed the College Entrance Examination but also had passed Cambridge School Certificate Examination. In this first lot was a woman student Josephine Nambooze, who, having passed School Certificate Examination, was admitted to a science course and later became the first African woman to qualify as a medical doctor at Makerere. She later became a professor of Medicine and has been the first woman to rise to a senior lectureship in the Medical School. Makerere now became the University College of East Africa. It had professional schools of Agriculture, Medicine, Veterinary Science, Education, faculties of Science and Arts and the School of Fine Art. There were about 200 students.

When the university college started preparing students for the University of London external degrees in science and arts, there was the problem of professional schools which were not covered by the special relationship with London University terms. There was, for example, no provision for these professional schools to prepare their students for external degrees of University of London in Medicine or Agriculture. Teachers in the Faculty of Science had the frustrating experience of having spent two years getting a promising student through the intermediate examination and when he was ready for entry to a degree course he would be lost to a professional school. Those who entered professional schools ended up with professional diplomas, but not degrees. The Medical School, particularly raised its standards and awarded a qualification, the licentiate in Medicine and Surgery (E.A.) which entitled its holder to registration as a medical practitioner in East Africa. This qualification was recognised by the General Medical Council of Great Britain in 1958. In the same year, the degrees of B.Sc. (Agric.) and B.Sc. (Econ.) were introduced.

In 1961, Makerere ceased to be Makerere College, the University College of East Africa, and became Makerere University College, since now the Royal College, Nairobi had the same status and relation with the University of London as Makerere. After that, in response to the East African's manpower requirements, and as a result of the expansion of advanced-level work at secondary schools, the University College grew considerably in numbers of students, teachers, facilities and variety of courses.

The Rise of Nairobi University

The earliest institution meant to provide higher education in Kenya was what was known in those days as the Royal Technical College of East Africa and was situated in Nairobi. Its establishment followed the recommendation of a committee under the chairmanship of Mr. G.P. Willoughby in 1949 that, Kenya Government set up a technical and commercial institute in Nairobi (a) to provide full-time and part-time instruction for courses leading to the Higher National Certificate (Britain) and (b) to prepare matriculated students through full-time study for university degrees in engineering and allied subjects not provided at Makerere. The Willoughby committee, in making the recommendation concerning higher levels of training, had European and Asian students in mind and made suggestions which display how little they know about East Africans' learning capacity. The committee stated:

> The institute has its primary aim to train European and Asian students. It will provide instruction in those practical trade skills which are being, or are to be taught to the African in trade schools now under the aegis of the Education Department. These courses should progress at speeds beyond the capability of the African and should be accompanied by higher theoretical study than would be appropriate for the African trade school. They would be calculated incidentally to prepare students for junior staff appointments where supervision of journeymen in various trades can be only efficient if the supervisor knows the elements and the theory of these trades though he   may not be highly skilled in them himself.

The East Africa High Commission assented to an Act establishing the college in 1954 after obtaining a Royal Charter for its establishment. The funds for its construction had come from Colonial Development and Welfare funds. Meanwhile Asians had donated funds and had erected another institution of higher learning called the Gandi Memorial Academy in honour and memory of the celebrated Indian leader through whose relentless efforts and personal sacrifice India had gained her independence. The two institutions were merged and started operating as one college in March 1956. It had the Departments of Arts, Commerce, Science, Engineering, Domestic Science, Architecture and Survey. The 3-year course led to special certificates and diplomas but not degrees.

Starting in 1958, there was such demand for degree courses with which Makerere the University College of East Africa at Makerere could not cope. The Higher Education in East Africa Working Party under Giffen consequently recommended that each territory should establish a university college. Following this recommendation the Royal Technical College began to conduct degree courses in 1961.

Like Makerere, it enjoyed a special relation with London University for whose external degrees in Arts, Engineering and Science it prepared its students. Its name was then changed to Royal College, Nairobi but it continued to prepare its students in Architecture, Art, and Commerce for diplomas. Furthermore, its students trained for admission to institutions like the Royal Institute of Chartered Surveyors, London, and its domestic science students whenever possible completed their courses at the University of Manchester.

In 1963, the Royal College Nairobi, by a change of name, became the University College, Nairobi and with the formation of University College, Dar-es-Salaam and the already existing Makerere University College the University of East Africa was established with the 3 territorial university colleges as constituent colleges. The pattern of organisation was like that of Makerere: There was a college council, the principal and other officials serving on it as ex-officio members. Other bodies such as the Inter-University Council of London, Gandhi Memorial Academy and the Kenya Chamber of Commerce were represented. Faculties headed by deans characterised the college.

Until 1971, the college was the only one of the three constituent colleges of the University of East Africa providing degree courses in Engineering Science.

The University College, Dar-es-Salaam

This started on a small scale with a law school and was housed in temporary buildings but it rapidly progressed that by 1966, it stood on a beautiful campus and had nearly 1,000 students.

The University of East Africa 1963-1970

The University of East Africa, a multi-national institution with Makerere University College, University College Nairobi and University College Dar-es-Salaam as constituent colleges began to operate in 1963. It was charged by its Act, 1962, with the "responsibility for university education within East Africa," and was required to "co-operate with governments or other appropriate bodies in the planned development of higher education and, in particular, to examine and approve proposals for new faculties, new departments, new degree courses or new subjects of study submitted to it by the constituent colleges".

Furthermore, the University of East Africa was given the responsibility for the admission of students to the three constituent colleges, to examine them and to award degrees, diplomas and certificates to candidates who passed its examinations. Put in fewer words, the task given to the university was to co-ordinate the academic activities, co-operate with the three sovereign states in providing high level manpower so urgently needed, and at the same time watch the development of each college so as to ensure the best use of the limited financial resources available then.

Some people have wondered why three sovereign states set up a federal university when they had no intention to have a political federal association for example. We guess that one of the reasons for the federal association of the colleges might have been that, since the special relationship with the University of London had been severed, the degrees and awards for which colleges prepared students would have more international reputation if awarded by one central university senate made up of representatives from individual colleges and, using external examiners in assessment of work presented by candidates. If it is true this was one of the reasons, there cannot be much quarrel with it because as the reader may be aware, in the world of learning there is no place for a degree that becomes unrecognised beyond the boundaries of the State where it is obtained.

The university awarded its degrees and brought to the end the era of London University external degrees for which its constituent colleges had previously been preparing their students. It maintained high standards and co-operated with universities overseas when recruiting staff. Its headquarters were in Kampala, Uganda.

An event of great importance in its early life was when in October 1963, the University of East Africa governments were invited to participate in a conference held at Lake Como, in Italy, sponsored by private and governmental aid agencies in Great Britain, America, Federal Republic of Germany, the World Bank, the Organisation for Economic Co-operation and Development and UNESCO. The purpose of the meeting was for the donors and recipients to draw up a 3-year development plan (1963-1966) for the university, based on funds donors would be able to make available and also on projection for staff. Two things about the plan deserve to be seriously noted. First, the university's capital and other requirements in the plan period were £3.85m. (Shs. 77million) and some donors were unable to commit themselves to specific sums although they showed interest. Secondly, the plan avoided a duplication of professional faculties by making the following allocation:-

Agriculture and Medicine	:	Makerere University College
Architecture, Engineering and Veterinary Science	:	University College Nairobi
Law	:	University College Dar-es-Salaam.

Some of the Problems of the University

A year after the Como Conference the university already had financial problems. Of the original £3.85m for capital requirements, £2m had not yet been received. Furthermore, it became evident that following the 1964 Creaser Report on Entrance Levels and Degree Structures, the number of students would rise and consequently more teaching facilities, staff and student residential accommodation would be needed. And in circumstances of risen costs, more funds than originally estimated would be needed.

To meet the urgently needed capital requirements, each government started working alone to get funds. Tanzania used some of its development loan from Britain to finance development at the University College, Dar-es-Salaam. Uganda requested the British Ministry of Overseas Development for a £692,000 grant to erect extra student and staff accommodation and a cafeteria in connection with the planned expansion of the Medical School. This failed and the Uganda government therefore, decided to raise the funds from her own resources. The university kept going despite financial problems, but as time went on, with nationalism rising higher and higher and each State making its own extensive national plans for education and manpower, the continuation of the University of East Africa became more and more uncertain.

It became weak particularly regarding steering the way in the area of development at constituent colleges. In the last quarter of 1964 there was intense speculation that Ugandan Authorities might unilaterally upgrade Makerere to University status at the end of the triennium in 1967. This speculation created an atmosphere of uncertainty over the two questions namely, whether the University of East Africa would exist for another triennium (1967-70) and whether in the face of uncertainty further development planning should be undertaken at all. Bernard de Bunsen, the vice chancellor, tried indirectly to get answers to these questions. He prepared a memorandum which he sent to colleges and governments in November 1964 asking them to indicate (i) whether they thought the powers of the university ought to be strengthened or modified and (ii) how long they thought the university should continue.

Kenyan and Tanzanian governments and colleges wanted the university to go on and to see its powers strengthened. Makerere, on the other hand, wanted to see the planning powers of the university taken over by colleges. Its main function to be the awarding of degrees and the guaranteeing of academic standards.

The reply from the Ugandan authorities did not come until at the university council meeting of May 20 1965. The government stressed that priorities in each country varied since the needs of each country were different. Furthermore, for a federal university to veto any government project was "sheer interference in the independent development of the country." The Tanzania representative's reaction to the Uganda statement was put in uncompromising terms in which it was stated that nationalisation of Makerere by Uganda's authorities (if it happened), would be incorrect, as Makerere College had been, for example, financed by British grants to serve all East Africa.

Despite the exchange of differing views at the meeting, and a resolution which recommended that the Uuniversity continues and that a review of its planning functions be undertaken, still, the future of the University of East Africa remained undecided. Starting in 1965, action taken by State governments concerning higher education, and without the agreement of the university, brought the date of its dissolution very much forward. For instance, Uganda upgraded Kampala Technical College to handle professional engineering courses. This obviously contravened the University of East Africa's arrangements for sharing professional schools and faculties between the three states as shown earlier in this account.

Yet, on the other hand, Uganda as an independent State needed to start producing professional engineers at home. In 1965, when it appeared to Makerere that the University Development Plan, which allowed Marerere £300,000 for the period 1964-67, spelt a halt to her expansion concern was shown in no uncertain terms, and this at once caused strain to the university. Kenya's White Paper on African Socialism 1965 which indicated that Kenya's national plans rather than East African requirements, would determine the future development of University College Nairobi, added further strain and stress to the university. The real blow came in July 1967 when Kenya decided to have a Faculty of Medicine in Nairobi. This step could also be justified on the grounds that it is difficult to see how Makerere Medical School, which had then facilities for up to 120 students only, could perform the task of giving East Africa the number of doctors needed in the 1960s and 1970s. In fact, even after the establishment of medical schools at Dar and Nairobi, East Africa was badly short of doctors in 1973. That the break-up of the University of East Africa did not come before 1970 is surprising for by 1968, each constituent college was already more or less acting as if separate.

On 1 July 1970, the University of East Africa slid into history and its constituent colleges became three separate fully-fledged universities. Its achievements can be summarised as follows:-

1. Through aid provided by the Ford Foundation the university maintained a scheme of exchange of staff for short periods to teach or do research at sister university colleges.

2. In its first three years of existence the university had funds which enabled teachers of certain subjects at the constituent colleges to meet periodically and review syllabuses and discuss problems of development.

3. Through the councils for Agricultural Education, Medical Education and Veterinary Education, which the university had created contacts with practitioners, and policy makers who were members of the councils were maintained. There was thus a dialogue between the university and the governments.

The Universities since 1970

Makerere University, Kampala, University of Nairobi and the University of Dar-es Salaam as separate entities have been on the move since 1970. Makerere has added a faculty of technology and faculty of veterinary science to the establishment and has for the first time in its history a Ugandan Professor of

Physics. The Faculty of Education has new courses that have given the long desired variety and a new look to its education programme. The department of Music, Dance and Drama is not only run by highly qualified African musicians and dramatists but shows determination to have a wide impact on schools particularly. The Post-graduate hall of residence, opened in 1971, is an indication of the rising numbers of students pursuing higher degrees. Nairobi by 1974 had, according to the 1970-74 plan, 3,443 undergraduates and up to 488 medical students. The latest development has been the raising to university college status of Kenyatta College which hitherto has been a teachers' college producing non-graduate teachers. Kenyatta University now prepares students for degrees awarded by the University of Nairobi. The establishment of the Faculties of Agriculture, Journalism and Law has been a part of the 1970-74 development plan. Dar-es-Salaam's Faculty of Medicine is going strong and the overall enrolment of undergraduates has risen. The three universities maintain a high standard and entry into any one of them is very competitive. They co-operate in areas of interest through the Inter-University Council of East Africa. Admission to any of the universities is open to any East African who satisfies the entrance requirements irrespective of where he or she comes from.

Lastly they have all gone along way in Africanisation of their members of staff.

Note

1. The Willougby Committee on Technical Education in Kenya, Government Printer Nairobi, 1950.

28

Miscellaneous and Conclusion

Centralized Control

Education in East Africa as a whole has been and continues to be highly centralized. Each sovereign state has continued to exercise legal and financial control. School inspection, and a national system of examinations has further signified the highly centralized control. There has been no significant indication in the direction of decentralisation.

Foreign Aid

None of the East Africa states has been able to do without foreign aid by way of money and technical assistance in the course of educational development since independence. The aid given to higher education has already been mentioned although not in much detail. There has also been considerable aid to non-university education. Many secondary schools owe their existence or expansion where buildings already existed, to foreign aid.

At the pace, and on the scale of development of education has been undertaken, recourse to foreign aid was just unavoidable. Indeed, the 1970 – 1974 Kenya Development Plan states that half of the country's capital needs in the four years will have to be financed by foreign loans and grants. The reference to Kenya is here being used as an example of what is true of the remainder of East Africa.

Finance apart, foreign aid came to East Africa in the form of technical assistance whose most memorable aspects was the Teachers for East Africa Scheme. Under the two schemes, sponsored by Britain and U.S.A., expatriate teachers came out to East Africa to help teach in secondary schools and teacher colleges. Mention should be made of programmes of volunteers under which again teachers have come to East Africa to teach. It would be unprofessional and dishonest not to give these teachers credit for their contribution.

Adult Education

From the end of the Second World War, the colonial administrators began to lay a great stress on out-of school education, which was known at first as "mass education" and later on as "adult education". The departments of education the departments of information, the department of community development and lay a great stress on out-of school education, which was known at first as "mass education" and later on as "adult education". The departments of education the departments of information, the department of community development and the British Council involved themselves very much in this work. At a higher level, Makerere University College established the department of Extra-Mural Studies in 1953. This department set up centres all over East Africa manned by resident tutors who were responsible for putting on weekly classes and short courses in towns and in large rural centres. Various government departments and voluntary organisations also began work at various stages in their own particular spheres.

The courses involved mostly two groups of people; those who had never been to school and those who had been to school. The former group was particularly engaged in learning how to read and write because it was felt that in a world where the written word meant so much, at least as many people as possible should be given the skill of reading and writing. The latter group concentrated normally on improving their knowledge in subjects that would better their prospects as employees especially in government departments by passing prescribed examinations. Courses for the latter group were conducted in urban areas and were usually successful. Classes were held in the evenings and people who wanted to attend them had free time to do so after office work. Courses of Kiswahili, Arabic, English, typing and book-keeping were generally successful.

There was much less success in the rural areas where people tended to be cultivators, fishers and carpenters or were employing themselves in other innumerable activities. Their work tended to occupy them all day long and they would find it hard to drop their work in the evenings to attend classes (mainly literacy) for men and domestic crafts and home management for women. Secondly such people did not see immediate benefit out of attendance. What used to happen was that centers opened to run such courses obtained enthusiastic attendance for a few weeks and then numbers began to dwindle until the centres were gradually closed for lack of attendance.

After independence adult education campaign did not stop. There was even a gradual increase in literacy and remedial and promotional courses. The above general pattern remained in operation.

Residential courses are held at several rural training for staff in various parts of a region at district level. In-service training for staff members are also held at training centres. Technical and vocational work is generally under the care of various ministries, and it provides evening classes in certain examination subjects in the larger towns where there is a demand for them.

The ministries doing the work of community development actively run literacy campaigns and award certificates to those people who attended them teach literacy. YMCA and some other voluntary organisations also help in various courses which are beneficial in a society. These activities such as film shows, radio talks, informal talks, debates, concerts, festivals and exhibitions, make up the present pattern of adult education in East Africa.

Definitely the work is already of a certain magnitude, but it is not enough in its efficiency and in its power to reach many people. It also needs more co-ordination in terms of national needs. The exercise should not reach only a few people while millions go uncatered for by any of the organised educational activities. This of course brings in the problem of staff and money the latter being in very much short supply. Manpower to run such courses is fortunately very much abundant only that it needs organisation and direction.

Conclusion

Education has played an important role in the development of East Africa since the beginning of closer contact with the rest of the world. There have never been laws to force children to go to school. Throughout the period covered in this book to all children of school age would have liked and do like to go to school if opportunities are available. Schools have always been full to over capacity. All students who have taught in East Africa have been favourably impressed by the East Africans' eagerness to learn.

Looking back, the missionaries, the colonial administrators and directors of education have a claim to make to the contribution to the progress made. Then, since independence the remarkable progress made should give us satisfaction. Yet there is actually no room for complacency for whether we like it or not there is a crisis in East African Education. By saying this, we are in no way suggesting that education in East Africa is collapsing or is in a state of decay; far from this, it is rapidly expanding. The term "crisis", as we are using it here, is meant to underline firmly the need to take stock of the situation, the need to appreciate the pressing need and the urgency to understand and prepare for the quantitative and qualitative changes that the technological revolution which is sweeping the world call for, as far as East Africa is concerned.

At independence, education was not only a matter of finding in the shortest possible time, qualified men to hold position of responsibility. It was more than that. It was a faith in the "magic" of education. Leaders of independent East Africa believed sincerely that investment in education would, among other things, generate employment. They again rightly held it as a right for all citizens. Thus when ministers of education form East Africa and other African states met in Addis Ababa in 1961 under the sponsorship of UNESCO, one of their epoch-making resolutions was the achievement of universal primary education by 1980. It was believed that this target could be achieved by increasing primary school enrolment by five percent yearly.

One of the findings of a study conducted by UNESCO just before 1968, was that generally, in developing countries, of which East Africa is one, public expenditure on education had risen on the average by 12.5 per cent a year and this was found to be much higher than the rate in the rise of the national income in each country. Economists have not failed to point out that if that rate is maintained it would be impossible to avoid spending less and less on investment on other development projects which are also vital.

Despite all the efforts and the tremendous rapid progress made, studies carried out seven years after Addis Ababa showed (OAU/UNESCO Nairobi Education Conference Papers 1969) that the rate of increase in enrolment was not yet anywhere near 5 per cent. It was 1.5 per cent. As of 1980, the target date comes nearer and nearer and the inevitable conclusion one has reluctantly to draw is this, that universal primary education is likely to be attained much later than that date. Uganda only a few years ago embarked on a universal primary education scheme. Where the government pays tuition for a maximum of four children per family.

Without trying to sound alarmist, although targets in secondary and university education have been much surpassed, and this is comforting, yet the output of the men most needed in a technological age namely, scientists and technicians is inadequate. And as circumstances have demonstrated on some occasions, it is idle to depend on expatriate sources. This and other problems give rise to the crucial question: What is to be done? Like many other people, our minds turn to what has been said over and over again, that there must be continual adjustment of school and university programmes if we are to benefit from the technological revolution.

Programmes are needed at secondary school level, designed to create a technical cadre of East Africans who can understand and make use of the terrific epoch of scientific discovery through which the world is rapidly passing. Methods of rote learning in school must go. Reform of the education systems which is ever on the lips of men in charge of providing education must not be taken lightly and must be translated into action. The question that is ever baffling is how do we do it effectively? To answer this question, curriculum designers are at work all over East Africa, efforts are being made to teach in new Mathematics and Science in a new way (hence the new terms like New Math, School Science Project). The sad part of the story is that in many cases this vital work is being done by men whose homes are not in East Africa and could go any time. Obviously, the involvement of East Africans is urgent. While we must make continual contacts with people concerned with education, we must aim at achieving self-reliance in promoting school system and in drawing up meaningful plans for further development of education with particular reference to the already mentioned technological revolution in which we are caught up. All those who have had opportunity of schooling must spontaneously involve themselves in the battle against illiteracy.

In conclusion, we would like to state that the struggle and efforts that have given us a record of achievement since independence in the area of education, of which we are proud, should continue relentlessly and without compromising the objectives, i.e. more and more real scientists, technicians and a near a hundred per cent majority of literate East Africans before the close of the century.

REFERENCES

Papers

The Phelps-Stokes Report 1923-4, J. Lewis ed.

Reports of the Education Department and the Ministry of Education 1925-68, Government Printer, Entebbe.

Report on Proceedings of the Legislative Council 1926, Government Printer, Entebbe.

The Laws of Uganda, 1927, 1959, Government Printer, Entebbe.

Education in Uganda 1940 (the Thomas Education Committee 1940), Government Printer, Entebbe.

African Education in Uganda. 1953 (the de Bunsen Report Government Printer, Entebbe, 1953).

The Economic Development of Uganda, International Bank for Reconstruction and Development, Government Printer, Entebbe, 1961.

The Teachers' Salary Report (the Lawrence Report), Government Printer, Entebbe, 1962

Education in Uganda, the Report of the Uganda Commission, Government Printer, Entebbe 1963.

Proceedings of the Uganda National Assembly, Vol. 22, Government Printer, Entebbe, 1963.

Subsidiary Legislation, Statutory Instruments, No. 224, 1969. Uganda Education Act 1970, Government Printer Entebbe, 1970.

Kenya Education Act 1970.

Proceedings of Tanganyika Legislative Council 1926, Dar-es-Salaam Government Printer.

Proceedings of Tanganyika Legislative Council 1958, Dar-es-Salaam 1958.

Ominde, Kenya Education Commission 1963 Part I and Part II, Nairobi Government Printer.

Makerere University College Reports 1961-70 Makerere Kampala.

East African Authority: Working Party on Higher Education in EA. Report submitted to the East African Authority at Arusha, January 31, 1969 (Nairobi 1969).

F. C.A. Cammaerts: "Priorities for the preparation of secondary teachers in Kenya". *East Africa Journal.* U.6. Vol. II November 1969.

Kenya: Board of Adult of Education. Triennal Report March 1969 Nairobi, Government Printer 1969.

Tanzania: Ministry of National Education 1969-74. Dar-es-Salaam.

H.M.R. Hawse: The Planning of School Curriculum in Uganda. M. Phil. In Education thesis, University of London 1969.

T. Watson: A History of Church Missionary Society. High Schools in Uganda; 1900-1924. Ph.D. thesis, University of East Africa 1969.

Books

Oliver, R: (1965) *The Missionary Factor in East Africa,* Longmans.

Tucker, A. R.: (1911) *Eighteen Years in Uganda and East Africa,* London Edward Arnold.

Welbourn,. F. B: (1965) *East African Christian,* Oxford University Press.

J. C. Ssekamwa, S. M. E. Lugumba: (1973) *Educational Development and Administration in Uganda 1900-1970.* Longmans Uganda.

E. Stabler: (1969) *Education since Uhuru, the schools of Kenya*, Middletown, Coun. Wesleyan, University Press.
W. A. Dodd: (1969) *Education for Self-Reliance in Tanzania: a study of its vocational aspects*, New York, Teachers College Press.
Cameron John: (1969) *The Development of Education in East Africa*, New York, Teachers College Press.
Jolly R: (Editor) (1969) Education *in Africa, research and action*, Heinemann Educational Books.
Anderson J: (1970) *The Struggle for the School*, Longmans, London.
Resnick J. N. (Ed.) (1971) *Tanzania: Revolution by Education*, Longmans Tanzania.
Ssekamwa J. C. A: (1971) *Sketch Map History of East Africa*, Hulton Educational Publications, England.
Ssekamwa J. C. (Ed.): 1971) *Readings in the Development of Education in East Africa*, Makerere University Kampala.

Tengeru
Teso College, Aloet
Thika Technical and Trade School
Thogoto Rural Training Centre

Index

Adult education 80, 140, 143, 145, 177, 178, 179
Advisory Council on African Education 12, 22
African 2-7, 9, 11, 12, 14, 15, 16, 17, 18, 19, 20-26, 27, 28-30, 32, 33, 34, 35, 36, 37, 38, 39, 40, 43, 47, 48, 50, 52, 53,55,56, 58, 60, 63, 64, 65, 72, 73, 74, 75, 76, 79, 80, 82, 84, 86, 90, 96, 97, 98, 99, 101, 102-105, 108, 109, 111-114, 125, 133, 134, 135, 137, 140, 141, 143, 144, 145, 150, 158, 162, 169, 174, 176, 178, 184
  Institute of the Church of God 3
  School Teachers Association (ASTA) 79
African Education Ordinance (1927). 94, 96 *See also* education ordinance (1938) 14, 52, 55, 168
Agali Awamu 81
Agricultural 4, 5, 6, 13, 15, 26, 27, 28, 44, 46, 51, 56, 59, 65-67, 69, 70, 90, 91, 92, 93, 97, 107, 115, 116, 117, 118, 120, 122, 126, 130, 157, 157
  College 27
  Education 4, 6, 26, 27, 28, 46, 65, 66, 115, 117, 176
  Education officer 27
  Schools 4, 27, 67
Agriculture 5, 6, 14, 22, 26, 27, 28, 36, 37, 44, 45, 46, 51, 52, 55, 65, 66, 67, 68, 86, 90, 99, 106, 113, 115, 116, 118, 125, 126, 130, 134, 144, 161
  and Technical Education 26
Anglican Church 8, 43, 74, 79
Asquith Commission 169

Beecher, Archdeacon 22
Beecher 19, 21, 22, 23, 26, 28, 34
  Committee of 1949 22
  Report of 1949 19, 28
  Ten-Year Development Plan 21
British Council 135, 177

Cambridge School Certificate 15, 23, 33, 36, 55, 104, 106, 134, 135, 157, 158, 167, 170
  Examination 15, 23, 33, 55, 106, 157, 170
Castle E.B. 149
Castle Education Commission 149, 150
  Recommendations 150
  Report 151
Catholic Teacher's Guild (CTG) 81
Central 5, 11, 13, 18, 19, 20, 21, 27, 37, 42, 48, 49, 51, 52, 63, 65, 87, 90, 92, 93, 95, 96, 105, 111, 151, 152, 157, 172
  Education Committee 103, 115, 118
  Schools 5, 48, 51, 52, 87, 90, 92, 93, 94, 95, 96
Centre for Continuing Education at Makerere 161
Church Missionary Society 2, 183
Church of Scotland Mission 2, 9
City and Guilds examinations 30, 135
Colonial Development and Welfare Fund 135
Compulsory Education Decree of 1921 138
Consolata Fathers 3
Creaser Report 173
Curriculum 26, 28, 41, 49, 51, 52, 54, 57, 69, 71, 97, 102, 121, 122, 130, 131, 140, 150, 156, 157, 158, 159, 161, 169, 182, 183
  Development Centre 161
  Reform 156

Dar-es-Salaam 85, 86, 89, 93, 94, 101, 103, 104, 107, 109, 118, 136, 163, 167, 172, 173, 183
  Education Conference 85
  Technical College 163
  Technical Institute 109
  University College Dar-es-Salaam 172, 173. *See also* Dar-es-Salaam
De Bunsen Bernard 60, 61, 62, 63, 174, 183
  Committee 61, 62, 63
  Report 183
De La Warr Commission 15, 104, 169
Department of education 4, 7, 29, 33, 43, 47, 48, 51, 52, 54, 55, 59, 63, 69, 92, 93, 103, 104, 106, 112, 113, 115, 123, 124, 125, 148
  Annual report 29
  Annual Report. *See also* education department report
District Education Board Ordinance, 1934 13

East Africa 2, 3, 5, 15, 16, 17, 24, 29, 31, 32, 33, 53, 54, 72, 84, 86, 95, 108, 109, 113, 115, 120, 131, 136, 139, 140, 144, 146, 154, 167, 168, 170 171, 172, 173, 174, 175, 176, 177, 178, 179, 180, 182, 183, 184
  Certificate of Education (EACE) 155
  Examinations Council 159
East African Army 56
  Education Corps 56
  Headquarters 56
Education 2, 4, 7, 9, 11, 12, 13, 14, 16, 17, 18, 19, 22, 23, 24, 26, 28, 29, 31, 32, 33, 36, 38, 39, 41, 42, 44, 46, 47, 48, 49, 50, 51, 54, 55, 56, 59, 60, 62, 63, 64, 65, 68, 71, 72, 75, 77, 79, 84, 85, 86, 87, 89, 92, 93, 94, 95, 96, 97, 100,
  Administration, Control and Supervision of Education 12
  Department Report 116
  Director of education 3, 4, 6, 9, 11, 13, 14, 16, 26, 35, 47, 48, 49, 50, 51, 53, 56-58 60, 61, 62, 64, 73, 85, 87, 89, 90,

94, 96, 99, 100, 106, 120, 121, 122, 136, 138, 149
  in the War Period 16
  Local Authorities and 63
  Missionary Contribution to 44
  Native Education 48
  Native education. *See also* Native of girls 62, 167
  of Muslim 59, 65, 79, 135, 151, 112, 152
  policy and administration 11, 32, 58, 86-88, 97, 125, 152, 153
  System 3, 11, 17, 18, 20, 23, 34, 36, 40, 41, 43, 49, 50, 51, 55, 65, 67, 68, 71, 77, 95, 101, 104, 115, 121, 125, 128, 129, 136, 137, 141, 144, 149, 150, 163
Educational 3, 4, 7, 8, 9, 10, 11, 12, 17, 19, 21, 22, 24, 28, 31, 34, 37, 42, 43, 44, 45, 47, 51, 54, 55, 56, 58, 59, 60, 63, 64, 65, 68, 69, 73, 74, 77, 78, 80, 83, 86, 87, 90, 95, 97, 100, 101, 102, 103, 105, 106, 107, 108,
  Development since independence, Ordinance 11, 166, 177
  (1924) 11
Education Ordinance 12, 13, 48, 56, 59, 60, 62, 64, 94, 96, 163
  (1927) 56, 94, 96
  (1931) 12, 13
  (1942) 56, 59, 60, 62
  (1962) 163
  Act 1963 153
  for Self-Reliance 163, 166, 184
Education policy 11, 32, 58, 86, 87, 96, 124, 125, 152, 153
  in British Tropical Africa 87, 97
Elementary 3, 13, 14, 17, 26, 48, 51, 53, 58, 59, 86, 88, 95, 121, 122, 167
  Certificate 13
  Schools 14, 58, 86

Female Education 75, 102, 112
Female education. *See also* Girls education
Ford Foundation 175
Fraser Nelson, J. 4
  Recommendations 4, 28

German Education System 85
Girls Boarding Schools 87
Government 3, 5, 7, 17, 19, 22, 27,
28, 29, 35, 37, 38, 39, 42, 47,
50, 54, 55, 58, 59, 60, 63, 65,
84, 85, 87, 89, 93, 94, 96, 97,
100, 104, 109, 112, 114, 116,
118, 120, 126, 128, 134, 135,
137, 151, 153, 171, 176, 183
Grants-in-aid 4, 7, 12, 1-111, 128,
132, 136, 138, 154, 165

Harambee 33, 144, 145
School Movement 144
High schools 4, 15, 30, 41, 48, 49, 150,
183
Higher School Certificate 33, 105, 132,
158, 159, 163
Holiday schools 88
Holy Ghost Fathers 2, 136

Imperial British East African Company 2
Independent Schools 2, 8, 9, 10, 11, 34,
35, 36
Kikuyu 9, 10, 36
Private 24, 73, 72 73, 74,
75, 136, 155, 156, 160
Infant Schools 129
Inspector of schools 9, 13, 43, 58, 61, 63,
149, 156, 157, 158, 161
Chief 47, 149, 156, 157, 158, 161
Inspection of Schools 43, 57, 62
Institute of Moslem Education 29
Inter-University Council 169, 172
Intermediate schools 24, 26, 27, 28,
36, 48
Isherwood Committee 100
Recommendations of 101, 103
Report 103
Jeanes 5
School 5
Teachers School 5
Junior Secondary Schools 7, 34, 55,
65, 71, 78, 79, 101, 104, 105, 152

Kampala Technical School 55, 56, 69
Kenya 2, 3, 5, 6, 7, 8, 9, 11, 12, 14,
15, 16, 17, 19, 20, 23, 24, 26,

27, 28, 29, 30, 31, 32, 33, 34,
36, 37, 38, 39, 51, 54, 72, 99,
109, 113, 132, 141, 142, 143, 145,
146, 147, 148, 149, 170, 172,
175, 176, 177, 183, 184
African Preliminary Examination
23, 33, 36
Asian Primary Examination 33
Education Commission 142, 183
European Primary Examination 33
National Union of Teachers (KNUT) 38
Polytechnic 30, 146
Kenyatta 148, 176
College 148, 176
University 148, 176
Kikuyu 2, 9, 10, 34, 36, 99
Educational association 10
Independent Schools Movement 9. *See
also* Independent Schools
Kiswahili 14, 51, 53, 54, 86, 89, 92, 95,
98, 99, 105, 119, 121, 122, 130,
131, 133, 163, 166, 178
Use of 53, 163
Koran schools 110, 111, 112, 119,
121, 126, 127, 128, 129, 134, 136, 138
Kwegyir, Aggrey Dr 42

Legislative Council 38, 48, 50, 73, 89,
90, 94, 98, 106, 107, 110, 118,
183
Local Native Councils 7, 8, 11, 13, 17,
18, 19, 20, 21, 23, 31, 34, 36, 37

Makerere 15, 16, 23, 26, 33, 37, 40,
44, 48, 52, 53, 55, 56, 58, 60,
67, 68, 82, 101, 102, 104,
105, 109, 113, 132, 135, 150, 154,
156, 159, 161, 162, 166, 167,
168, 169, 170, 171, 172, 173,
174, 175, 176, 177, 183, 184
College 15, 16, 33, 37, 48, 53, 55, 60,
101, 104, 113, 167, 168, 169,
170, 175
College Act 169
College Council 168
College Ordinance 168
Entrance Examination 23, 104
University 55, 132, 150, 161, 162,

166, 170, 172, 173, 176, 177, 183, 184
University College 132, 150, 170, 172, 173, 177, 183
Maternity schools 42
Mau Mau 34, 35, 36
Middle schools 96, 101, 104, 105, 106, 115, 116, 117, 163
Mill Hill Fathers 2, 41, 59
Ministry of Education 19, 65, 112, 142, 144, 145, 148, 152, 153, 154, 155, 161, 165, 183
Missions 2, 3, 4, 8, 9, 11, 13, 14, 15, 37, 40, 42, 45, 46, 47, 48, 49, 50, 59, 65, 70, 74, 81, 86, 87, 89, 93, 95, 111, 124, 129, 136, 151
Schools 7, 8, 9, 43-47, 50, 51, 55, 58, 73, 77, 86, 87, 89, 93, 95, 96, 101, 136
Missionaries 2, 3, 4, 6, 7, 8, 11, 12, 16, 18, 22, 40, 41, 42, 43, 44, 45, 46, 48, 52, 55, 69, 74, 77, 81, 87, 93, 94, 95, 111, 120, 136, 180

Nairobi 17, 22, 29, 30, 38, 39, 71, 109, 134, 142, 146, 148, 170, 171, 172, 173, 175, 176, 180, 183
Nairobi University 170
National Education System 144, 151
Native 5, 7, 8, 9, 11, 13, 18, 19, 20, 21,.23, 31, 32, 34, 35, 37, 86, 90, 91, 92, 101, 165
Administration schools 90, 91, 92, 96, 112
Affairs 5, 8, 38
Commissioner for 5, 8
Councils 7, 8, 11, 13, 18, 19, 20, 21, 23, 31, 32, 34, 36, 37 *See also* Local Native Councils
Native Authority Ordinance 90
Education 47
Native education. *See also* Native Industrial Training Depot 28
Normal schools 41, 48, 51, 53, 58

Ominde, S.H. 142
Ominde Education Commission (1963) 142
After the 144

Peace Corps 154
Phelps-Stokes 6, 41, 42, 43, 44, 47, 87, 183
Commission 6, 41, 42, 43, 44, 47
Fund 42
Primary 13, 14, 17, 18, 19, 26, 28, 32, 33, 41, 52, 54, 70, 71, 75, 77, 78, 82, 103, 105, 112, 114, 115, 120, 122, 126, 128, 129, 130, 132, 134, 135, 136, 141, 148, 150, 155, 156, 157, 166
Certificate 13, 14
Leaving Examination 33, 75, 78, 155, 157
Lower 13, 15, 131
Schools 7, 14, 15, 16, 17, 18, 19, 20, 21, 23, 24, 26, 27, 28, 51, 52, 54, 55, 65, 66, 69, 70, 74, 76, 77, 78, 79, 82, 102, 104, 109, 112, 116, 126, 128, 129, 130, 132, 133, 134, 135, 136, 143, 151, 157, 166
School Curriculum 156
Primary education 21, 22, 23, 32, 33, 34, 60, 61, 62, 63, 68, 69, 93, 101, 109, 128, 132, 133, 143, 145, 151, 161, 165, 166, 167, 180, 181
Expansion of 17, 18, 167
Private Schools 15, 75, 107, 155
Rise of 72, 73
Protestant Mission board of education 3

Racial 3, 31, 32, 34, 72, 73, 75, 102, 108, 109, 110, 132, 144, 153, 159, 164
Systems of Education 108
Segregation 31, 72
Racialism 31
in Education 31
Royal Technical College Nairobi 71
Rural 5, 18, 27, 28, 36, 43, 70, 97, 101, 115, 116, 117, 120, 122, 125, 126, 131, 132, 135, 178, 184
Education 115, 120, 125
Education Policy 125
Training Centre 27, 36, 184

School 2, 3, 4, 5, 9, 11, 12, 13, 14, 15, 16, 17, 18, 22, 23, 24, 26, 27, 28, 29, 30, 31, 32, 34, 36, 37, 40, 41, 43, 45, 46, 47, 48, 49, 50, 51, 52, 53, 54, 55, 56,
Certificate 15, 22, 23, 24, 25, 29, 33, 36, 55, 71, 104, 105, 106, 132, 134, 135, 144, 148, 157, 158, 159, 163, 167, 169, 170
System 4, 11, 12, 14, 18, 30, 43, 45, 47, 55, 99, 104, 112, 139, 163, 182
Secondary 5, 7, 8, 12, 13, 14, 15, 16, 18, 19, 22-24, 25-30, 32, 33-36, 37, 41, 52, 53, 55, 56, 59, 60, 61, 62, 64-67, 69, 70-75, 77, 78, 79, 82, 96, 101, 102, 104-107, 110, 113, 122, 129, 131-136, 140, 141, 143, 144 145, 146, 148, 151, 152, 154, 155, 157-159, 161, 163, 166, 167, 168, 170, 177, 181, 182, 183
Education 8, 12, 13, 14, 15, 16, 19, 24, 26, 27, 33, 36, 61, 71, 72, 75, 79, 96, 101, 104, 105, 106, 110, 113, 122, 132, 140, 143-146, 148, 154, 155, 159, 168
School 12, 36, 15, 52, 78, 112, 113, 116, 141, 148, 157, 159
Secondary School 5, 13, 15, 32, 33, 36, 52, 60, 61, 63, 68, 69, 74, 76, 78, 79, 81, 101, 102, 104, 106, 107, 130, 131, 132, 133, 134, 136, 140, 141, 144, 145, 146, 151, 153, 155, 157, 158, 159, 160, 161-163, 166, 168, 180
Curriculum 157
Education 159
Boom in 159
Segregation in Education 32, 72
Seventh Day Adventists 3
Sub-elementary schools 14

Tanganyika Legislative Council 89, 118, 183
Teacher 5, 15, 16, 36, 37, 45, 48, 49, 51, 52, 54, 59, 61, 62, 70, 77, 78, 80, 82, 86, 91, 92, 95, 96, 99, 101, 102, 103, 105, 112, 113,

115, 116, 119, 121, 122, 125, 126, 128, 134, 140, 146, 147, 151, 152, 154, 156, 160, 161, 163, 168, 177
Education 36, 55, 134, 146, 147, 154, 160
Teacher education 16, 140, 146, 147, 160, 161, 167, 168
Training colleges 15, 62, 78, 82, 113, 114, 134, 146, 151, 154, 160, 161
Grade I 36, 37
Grade II 36
Grade III 154
Union 82
Teaching Service Commission 83
Technical 26, 28, 29, 30, 45, 55, 56, 60, 61, 65, 68, 69, 70, 71, 72, 107, 109, 114, 123, 134, 146, 151, 154, 161, 162, 163, 170, 171, 175, 176, 178, 184
College 29, 71, 109, 161, 162, 163, 170, 171, 175
Education 26, 28, 29, 65, 68, 71, 123, 134, 176
Technical education 11, 29, 45, 58, 61, 68, 69, 90, 143, 144, 146, 161
See also Agriculture and technical school 29, 31, 45, 55, 56, 51, 69, 134, 135, 167
Trade School 29, 135, 184
Trade school 29, 30, 31, 171

Uganda 2, 4, 6, 15, 24, 37, 40, 41-43, 45, 47, 50, 51, 53, 54, 55, 56, 59, 60, 61, 63, 64, 65, 68, 69, 72, 73, 74, 77, 78, 79, 80, 81-85, 99, 104, 107, 109, 113, 134, 135, 149, 150, 151, 152-154, 156, 161, 162, 173, 175, 181, 183
African Teachers Association (UATA) 80
Muslim Education Association (UMEA) 79
United Methodist Mission 2
United Missionary Conference for Protestant Missions 3

United Nations Mission to Tanganyika 117
Universal Primary Education 19, 32,
132, 180, 181
Universities 132, 136, 168, 173, 175, 176
Mission to Central African (UMCA) 136
Since 1970 176
University 55, 113, 132, 148, 149, 150,
161, 162, 166, 168, 169, 170, 171,
172, 173, 174, 175, 176, 177,
183, 184
College Nairobi 172, 173, 175. *See also*
Nairobi
East Africa 172, 173, 174, 175, 183

Vernacular 14, 48, 51, 54, 55, 82, 95, 96,
99, 153
Primary and Junior Teachers Union 32,
132, 180, 18182
Schools 48, 51, 54, 55, 95
Verona Fathers 59

Village schools 4, 5, 88, 92, 96, 122,
115
Vocational schools 16, 51
Volunteer Service Overseas 154

White Fathers 45, 59, 93
White Paper on Education in Tropical Africa
47
Willoughby Committee 29, 171
Willoughby, G.P. 170

Zanzibar 111, 119, 120, 121, 122-126,
128, 130- 132, 134-138
Education in 119, 137, 138
Education System 11, 54, 55, 75,
85, 95, 105, 107, 120, 141,
143, 151, 163
Zanzibar Teacher Training College 134